"Bravo! Dr. Jannot has written an incredible resource for families who are truly struggling to navigate raising children in our fast-paced, highly demanding modern world. *The Disintegrating Student* provides practical tools and easy-to-understand tips guiding parents in how to reconnect with and develop essential executive functioning skills in their children. I am excited to be able to reference this to families I see in my private practice who struggle with these issues everyday."
—Lisa Reid, LCSW, Essential Connections
    Counseling & Consulting

"If you're looking for real understanding of why your student might be struggling, that answer . . . can be found in *The Disintegrating Student*! Dr. Jannot manages to succinctly explain the pressures of societal expectations, teenage brain development, and the psychology of parenting styles and motivation in a way that helps create a full picture of what may be happening for your child, how to help overcome those obstacles, and maybe even adjust your own expectations without feeling like you're giving in. 'Successful' students are more than just good grades, and this book is a primer for creating a strong foundation for success."
—Krista Smith, organizational psychologist
    and mother of three (ages 16, 14, and 10)

"*The Disintegrating Student* will quickly become an essential guide for every student and parent working to survive and thrive in the current education environment."
—Carolyn Lambert, parent coach, Nathan's Waypoint

THE DISINTEGRATING STUDENT

STRUGGLING BUT SMART AND FALLING APART . . . AND HOW TO TURN IT AROUND

JEANNINE JANNOT, Ph.D.

CITADEL PRESS
Kensington Publishing Corp.
www.kensingtonbooks.com

CITADEL PRESS BOOKS are published by

Kensington Publishing Corp.
119 West 40th Street
New York, NY 10018

PUBLISHER'S NOTE
The stories shared by the author in this book are based on years of client interactions but are not based on any individual person. Any resemblance to persons, living or dead, or actual events is purely coincidental.

All Kensington titles, imprints, and distributed lines are available at special quantity discounts for bulk purchases for sales promotions, premiums, fundraising, educational, or institutional use.

Special book excerpts or customized printings can also be created to fit specific needs. For details, write or phone the office of the Kensington sales manager: Kensington Publishing Corp., 119 West 40th Street, New York, NY 10018, attn: Sales Department; phone 1-800-221-2647.

CITADEL PRESS and the Citadel logo are Reg. U.S. Pat. & TM Off.

ISBN-13: 978-0-8065-4132-7
ISBN-10: 0-8065-4132-8

First printing: August 2021

10 9 8 7 6 5 4 3 2

Printed in the United States of America

Electronic edition:

ISBN-13: 978-0-8065-4133-4 (e-book)
ISBN-10: 0-8065-4133-4 (e-book)

To my greatest teachers,
Ryan, Maddie, Jason & Kat

Contents

A Note to Parents

THE FOLLOWING ACCOUNT was written by a high school student:

> It's 6:00 a.m. on a Thursday and my alarm is blaring. I roll over to hit the snooze button. I was up until 2:00 a.m. doing homework, and if I could get just five more minutes . . .
>
> Just as I'm falling back asleep, Mom comes barging in. She probably had a tough time getting my little sister up, because she's in a bad mood. She practically yells at me to get up and asks about the overdue Honors English homework I was supposed to finish last night. I try to explain that I decided to finish my AP World History project instead, because it's worth more than a homework grade in a class I already have an *A* in. By the way she looks at me I can tell she's pissed. She tells me that I can't

use my phone until I finish all of the homework. I haven't even gotten out of bed yet
and I'm already in trouble. Great.

By the time I get out of the shower and
ready for school it's 7:20. I need to leave
for the bus by 7:30, so I'm rushing to pack
a lunch and get out the door when Mom
comes into the kitchen. She reminds me
again to finish the English homework,
and I'll admit I snapped at her because
I'm stressed about making the bus on time
and the eighty other things I need to do
when I get home from school. My flash of
attitude was the final straw for Mom, and
now I can't go to my best friend's house for
a sleepover on Friday. My friend and I had
been looking forward to this sleepover so
much because we've both been so busy with
homework that we just wanted to relax and
watch some TV.

This story is not unusual. If you are the parent of a
teenager, it may be all too familiar to you. In the years
I've spent coaching students, I have heard dozens of
variations of this scenario.

Promising anonymity, I asked a number of high
school students: "What do you wish your parents
understood better?" Here are some of their responses:

"School is much harder than you remember so don't pretend you get it because you don't."

"Don't compare us to our friends or family."

"I'll never be like [insert sibling name]. Just accept me for me."

"Always be proud of your child even if what they achieve is not what you expect from them. They try really hard each day and finding out that their best isn't enough is discouraging."

"Checking grades every night may not give us the best motivation."

"Mental health issues aren't the result of bad parenting, but it is bad parenting to be afraid to look for help for your kid because you don't want the public to know."

"Sometimes we do need time for our mental health."

"I wish my parents knew that telling a kid that they have no real problems just

> makes whatever issues they were hav-
> ing ten times worse."

> "We really do care. We are not lazy. We
> care so much it's scary."

That last statement brings a lump to my throat every time I think about it. Over and over (and over) again, I find that once-successful students who've practically given up, who *seem* as if they don't care anymore, really do care, a lot. In fact, they care so much that when they start to struggle academically, their caring morphs into anxiety and essentially paralyzes them into inaction. As their grades decline and their schoolwork piles up, their anxiety increases until they spiral out of control and completely fall apart. They become what I call a *Disintegrating Student*.

My concerns about the well-being of students began when I worked as a school psychologist, escalated as my own children went through school, and peaked when I started teaching psychology at a local university. I was surprised and dismayed by the struggles so many students face, in and out of the classroom. I came to realize that our primary and secondary school systems are a big part of the problem as the focus in education has shifted from the learning process to learning outcomes and products. I also came to realize that we are raising the most stressed out, psychologically fragile generation in history, and parents, educators, and society seem unable to help these kids, despite having the best intentions.

In order to help students be productive and well, I started my coaching practice, *The Balanced Student*, where I work with students (and parents) to assess what they've been doing well, understand areas where they need support, and develop the skills needed to succeed in today's academic world (and in life).*

Many students who are struggling academically feel that their parents don't understand or don't care about what they are going through. As a parent myself, I find this frustrating and disheartening. While it's true that parents may not understand everything that is happening, in my experience most parents care more than their children will ever know. That deep concern, and their search for understanding, is why parents bring their children to *The Balanced Student* in the first place—and it's likely the reason you're reading this right now. So if you take away only one thing from this book, I hope it is this: *The very fact that you are working so hard to help your child makes you a great parent.*

Of course, I plan to give you more information than just these words of encouragement! As noted, the final chapter of this book, "77 Tips to be Productive and Well,"

---

* You'll find many of these strategies in this book, especially the final chapter, "77 Tips to Be Productive and Well."

will give you practical strategies and tools that you can use to help your disintegrating student. But there is a reason these practical strategies are in the last chapter instead of the first. Imagine sitting down tomorrow evening with your struggling student and explaining a bunch of new study techniques they can use to bring their grades up.

Total success. Problem solved. Right?

More likely, it would lead to a repeat of many painful—and possibly explosive—exchanges you and your child may already have had. So before we talk about practical strategies, I want to help you understand the phenomenon of the disintegrating student, including the physical, developmental, and cultural forces that lead previously stellar students to fall apart, and the parenting styles and struggles that can contribute to it. As we go along, I'll share the experiences of disintegrating students and their families. The details of the stories will be altered to remove any identifying information. With the exception of my own children, everyone else mentioned represents a composite of clients I have worked with over the years.

Waiting until the end of the book to get to the "77 Tips to be Productive and Well" may be frustrating, I know. As loving, concerned parents, we all want to help our kids as quickly as possible. We want simple solutions, and we want them now! (And getting a little more peace and quiet at home would be great, too.)

But understanding *why* our supersmart students fall apart is critical to understanding how to help them.

Unfortunately, I can't tell you *exactly* what to do. In my experience there isn't one sure-fire approach that works for every student or family. Every disintegrating student is different, and what will work best for your child depends on your child's (and your) individual strengths and challenges.

While I can't give you a simple answer, I *will* help you find the answers you need.

THE
DISINTEGRATING
STUDENT

CHAPTER 1

What Is a Disintegrating Student?

I COINED THE TERM *disintegrating student* to help me more succinctly describe a type of student that I repeatedly encountered throughout my years of teaching and academic coaching. These students all had a history of outstanding academic achievement. Many were identified early on as being intellectually gifted. As elementary students, they loved school, completed homework in class or on the bus, and rarely needed to study for tests. They seemed to process and retain new information simply by being exposed to it. It was easy to parent these kids and a joy to teach them. No helicopter parenting was required!

And then, often without any apparent warning, some of the best and brightest of these conscientious, motivated kids seemed to fall apart, both academically and emotionally. Their parents typically didn't even realize that there was a problem until they noticed a decline in grades. It's not uncommon for that first "What's wrong, honey?" to trigger an emotional outburst. Often the students can't answer that question, either because they don't understand the problem themselves, or because their feelings about it are too complex to explain.*

I've worked with many disintegrating students similar to a sixth-grader I'll call Craig.

> Craig lived at home with his parents and his younger brother, Ted, a fourth-grader. The boys were close, but competitive, and they teased each other relentlessly. Craig was a fast learner who had always made good grades with very little effort and no need for outside help. Ted, on the other hand, struggled in school from the very beginning. In the third grade he was diagnosed with anxiety and Attention Deficit Hyperactivity Disorder (ADHD).
>
> Craig's grades started to slip. It was nothing lower than a B at first, but he dreaded

---

* Some disintegrating students may also have challenges related to Attention Deficit Hyperactivity Disorder, learning disorders, or mental health issues like anxiety. While highly intelligent, they are eventually further disadvantaged by their nontypical thinking and learning styles that conflict with their school learning environment.

his next report card. His parents suggested he work harder, but didn't really follow up, assuming that Craig would eventually get the hang of middle school. They were preoccupied with Ted's issues, and besides, Craig never needed or wanted any help with schoolwork anyway.

Sometimes Craig's parents would argue, and sometimes Craig would see his mom crying. Craig was worried about his mother and was angry with his little brother for needing so much attention. The boys' good-natured teasing gradually turned into something a little less friendly and more aggressive. This only made things worse for Craig's mom, who constantly reprimanded Craig for being mean to Ted.

Craig's feelings were all jumbled up. There was so much that was out of his control, yet he felt a lot of internal pressure to make everything right. He worried about his mother's stress and his parents' marriage. He resented the disproportionate amount of attention Ted got from his parents, but at the same time, for all their fighting, he loved his brother and knew that Ted needed the extra help. He understood that his parents were under a lot of pressure.

Middle school was hard and confusing.

He was having trouble keeping up with the challenging work, and he was kind of freaking out. Craig was stuck. He couldn't do the work, but he didn't want to ask for help either. He was hiding his struggles, but at the same time he was sad and mad that no one noticed or seemed at all concerned about the problems he was having. It wasn't just about trying harder; he'd tried as hard as he could, but it hadn't worked. He felt like no matter what he did, it wasn't nearly enough.

Craig wanted desperately to be the ideal son, brother, and student he had always been, able to handle whatever came his way, but he just couldn't do it any longer. He felt overwhelmed and powerless. He eventually gave up on school and quit trying, and his grades plummeted. Craig became a disintegrating student. He was still supersmart, but he was falling apart!

The types of issues facing Craig, and his response to them, are not uncommon among the disintegrating students I work with. Of course, there are many, many variables that determine whether a student disintegrates: intellectual ability, individual personality, coping mechanisms, social supports, and relationships with parents, teachers, and friends all play important roles.

As students encounter more (and significantly more difficult) schoolwork, they inevitably reach a point where they can no longer manage it easily. I call this the *rigor tipping point*. As grades begin to drop, negatively affecting their attitude and self-esteem, it creates a perfect storm of external and internal pressures, which causes some of the best and brightest students to fall apart.

In Craig's case, it wasn't a question of not being smart enough; he was. It wasn't a question of not trying hard enough; he most definitely did. Like most of the disintegrating students I've worked with, Craig was smart and wanted to do well, but he had a number of skill deficits and counterproductive habits that did not impact him until he reached his rigor tipping point.* And when they did impact him, he didn't ask for help.

The skill deficits and counterproductive behaviors that are common among disintegrating students are concentrated in seven areas:

---

* In my academic coaching experience, I have found eighth and tenth grades to be reliable rigor tipping points, as well as the second semester of the freshman year in college. However, this can happen anytime in a student's academic career.

- *Organization*—They have trouble keeping track of their belongings and can't find things when they need them. They forget things. Their backpacks are a mess. They have no system for keeping schoolwork and papers organized.

- *Time Management*—They don't know how to prioritize tasks or estimate the time they need to complete work. Most don't keep a calendar or schedule, and don't know how to. They procrastinate.

- *Study Habits and Skills*—They don't study in places, at times, or in a manner conducive to learning. Most don't know how to study, and some don't study at all. They don't know how to differentiate key ideas and concepts from less important information.

- *Mindset*—They have a negative attitude toward school. They avoid challenges. They get frustrated easily and often. They are hard on themselves. They may have a negative outlook on everything.

- *Stress*—They worry a lot. They complain about headaches and stomachaches and get sick a lot. They ask to stay home from school frequently. They may experience test anxiety.

- *Sleep*—They stay up way too late. They often have trouble falling asleep at night, and it's almost impossible to wake them up in the morning. They complain about fatigue and are more susceptible to getting sick. They frequently complain about being exhausted.

- *Screens*—They have trouble self-regulating their screen time. They spend a lot of time attached to their smartphones. They play video games for hours at a time. They spend more time interacting with people virtually than in person. They have difficulty transitioning off their screens when asked.

You may recognize some, possibly many, of these skill deficits and counterproductive behaviors in your own child. If you do, take comfort in the knowledge that you are not alone. The number of disintegrating students has grown significantly in recent years.

To understand why this has happened and what we can do to help get these students back on track, we first need to look at how the human brain develops, and the role that cultural and parental influences play in the lives of our children.

CHAPTER 2

Developmental Influences

THE ADOLESCENT BRAIN

To UNDERSTAND the disintegrating student, we must start with the basics of human brain development. Extensive neuropsychological research in the past two decades has revealed more—and more complex—changes in the developing brains of tweens, teens, and young adults than we ever suspected.

One of the astounding conclusions to emerge from this body of research is an extension of the age range of adolescence. Historically, adolescence was thought to occur during the teen years, ages 13 through 19, typically beginning with the onset of puberty and ending when children finished high school.

New research has shown what many parents already suspected—adolescent changes in the brain start earlier and are not complete until far later than originally thought. These findings, along with shifts in societal expectations, have led neuropsychologists to redefine the period of adolescence as occurring between the ages of 12 and 25, essentially doubling the amount of time our children spend in adolescence. And we now know that the changes that take place in the brain during this extended period of time are profound!

BRAIN PLASTICITY

Research has confirmed that a very young child's brain is exceptionally malleable and *plastic*, which means it will change and grow as a result of experience. It comes equipped at birth with over 100 billion neurons (nerve cells) ready to make all the connections needed to walk and talk and read and write and do everything else we learn over a lifetime. Each of these 100 billion neurons connects with 1,000 to 10,000 other neurons, making trillions of connections, all contained within the three pounds of *Wow!* that is the human brain.

Extensive study of infants has taught us that experience is the essential catalyst for this massive and intricate system of neurological connections. Give the young brain sensory input—sight, sound, taste, smell and touch—and it learns things at an incredibly rapid rate.

Unfortunately, we have all too much evidence that the opposite is also true: babies and children who experience isolation, neglect, and/or abuse are at high risk for developmental and intellectual delays and deficits. The good news is that this new understanding of the young brain's window of exceptional plasticity has helped researchers find effective interventions to help these children.

We also know that brains don't develop in a straight line, constantly adding new neural connections on top of all the old ones. In fact, to allow for healthy growth, our brains periodically remove weak and nonessential neural connections, a process called *neural pruning*. Just as in a garden, where pruning the overgrowth allows for further growth and expansion, neural pruning enables the human brain to develop and grow. Researchers have long known that the first neural pruning occurs around age two, after the development of language.

Brain-plasticity research has sparked a booming industry in developmental enhancement products. Stimulating mobiles, textured toys, classical music CDs and downloads, and so-called "educational" videos and games have become "must have" items to give our children a leg up in the cut-throat educational journey they must navigate.

While this so-called "Birth to Three" movement focused parents (and marketers) on our youngest children, we tended to ignore our teens, who continued to make their transitions to adulthood under the old assumption that the changes in their lives were all about hormones, and had little to do with physical changes in their brains. Fortunately, in the background, brain researchers continued their work, using breakthrough imaging techniques like *functional magnetic resonance imaging* (fMRI) to explore adolescent brain development. And the findings were game changing.

Even before the expansion in fMRI capabilities, researchers knew that the brain goes through a second neural pruning during adolescence. What they didn't know was that this pruning coincides with another highly malleable phase of brain development, where the brain takes on a plasticity similar to that found between birth and three. The research into this second phase of brain development has advanced our understanding of the brain by leaps and bounds—and also helped explain some idiosyncratic (and on occasion, idiotic) adolescent behavior.

COGNITIVE DEVELOPMENT

"What were you thinking?!" How many times have you asked your child some version of this question? If you're a typical parent, too many to count, though the number of times you got a satisfactory answer could probably be counted on the fingers of a closed hand.

It would be more informative, and more useful, to learn *how* they are thinking. According to Jean Piaget, the Swiss psychologist who pioneered cognitive developmental theory, at about the same time their bodies shift into adolescence, children's thinking shifts from being concrete and logical to being more flexible, hypothetical and abstract. It goes from "black and white" to "fuzzy and gray."

According to Piaget, we pass through four stages of cognitive development in our lives, with each stage represented by cardinal features in thinking: *sensorimotor, preoperational, concrete operational,* and *formal operational.*

We experience the *sensorimotor* stage through the first two years of life. At this stage, thinking is the product of integrating sensory information with our constantly changing motor capabilities. How do babies find out about something new? They touch. They grab. They stick things in their mouths (unless we get to it first!).

The second stage is *preoperational,* occurring between the ages of 2 and 7. This phase is highly egocentric, marked by intense inquisition and exploration that is often stymied by limitations in understanding. For example, a preoperational child understands symbolic representations, but not object constancy, a gap easily demonstrated through a classic "how many" conservation task. If you show a 4-year-old two graham cracker squares, then break one into two equal pieces and ask if the whole cracker and the broken cracker are the same amount, the child will say no. Why? Well, because they understand that two is more than one, but they are unable to conserve the underlying volume and mass to see that just breaking something in half doesn't change how much of it there is.*

The third stage, between the ages 7 and 11, is called *concrete operational*. During this stage, children's thinking is still quite concrete and literal, but they begin to understand the perspectives of others and can think in more logical terms. They easily recognize the constancy of volume and mass in conservation tasks, meaning they fully realize that they can't get more graham cracker simply by breaking a cracker in half and making two pieces out of it. If asked about this, their incredulous, often hilarious responses to being asked such an obvious question suggest they have no idea that they ever thought any differently.

The shift into the fourth and final stage of cognitive development, *formal operational*, occurs during middle and high school, usually around the age of 12. What is most remarkable about this stage is a new capacity to think in both abstract and hypothetical terms, giving our teens the opportunity to learn and think more deeply and profoundly. It's no coincidence that during the formal operational stage they start to ponder some of the big questions of life, sometimes becoming moody and morose in the process. At the same time, their

---

* A YouTube search for "conservation tasks" yields many informative and entertaining videos of children in the preoperational stage.

newly discovered ability to see situations and solutions from multiple perspectives gives them enhanced problem-solving skills.

The formal operational stage is transformative, but as part of that transformation, some significant regressions show up. The egocentric characteristics of the 2 to 7-year-old preoperational child reappear, but in a more complex form. Teens become aware of other perspectives, but a new self-consciousness gives them the feeling that those other perspectives are always focused on *them*. In psychology this is referred to as the *spotlight effect*, the sense people have that attention is being disproportionately directed at them. With my own children, I first noticed this when they began to "Shhh!" me in public places. They would whisper that everyone could hear me and that I was embarrassing them. Honestly, I cannot imagine talking any more softly, and most of the time no one else was even within earshot, but my rebuttals fell on deaf ears; they knew for certain that everyone was watching, listening, and judging.

For many years, our teens navigate through life feeling this way, that they are under constant, intense scrutiny from others. Teens put an incredible amount of pressure on themselves trying to live up to the opinions they *think* others have of them. They spend a disproportionate amount of time and energy thinking about and reliving things they've said and done with the absolute certainty that they are being evaluated, judged, and commented on by everyone they encounter. As adults, we recognize the painful irony; while our teens worry about what others—especially other teens—are thinking about them, those others are usually busy worrying about the exact same thing!

In addition to developing a hyperawareness of self during the formal operational stage, memory formation becomes more focused on details, giving increased significance to everyday events and experiences. Compare your own memories from high school with those of highly significant events in your life as an adult, like your marriage, the birth of a child, or a new job. You can recall these events, of course, but probably with far less clarity than the many seemingly insignificant (in retrospect) details you remember from adolescence, like your favorite sweater, that awful haircut, or the embarrassing thing you said to your crush that one time. (Come on. You remember.)

Information and experiences, even the most insignificant, being burned into the adolescent brain with such intensity is a good news/bad news situation. The good news is that, just as an infant and young child's brain is proficient at learning to walk and talk, an adolescent's brain is ready and able to absorb information at a time when they are facing new academic challenges and exploring new interests. It's great to see this in our kids.

The bad news is that the brain is an equal opportunity sponge that will soak in experiences both positive and negative. An adolescent's brain exposed to negative influences can easily internalize harmful thinking and behavior patterns. For example, adolescents with a history of alcoholism in their family may have a genetic vulnerability to the disease which is influenced by their unique experiences and exposure. Because the adolescent brain is so spongy and learns through experience, the younger someone starts drinking (exposure), the higher their risk of dependence and further substance use. And because the brain has learned addiction so well, the prognosis for recovery is poorer than those who begin drinking after adolescence.

EMOTIONAL DEVELOPMENT

Anyone who's parented a teenager can attest to the fact that they can be very emotional, and that they don't always exercise the best judgment. They aren't like this because they want to drive their parents crazy, even though it may seem that way at times. They are like this for the simple, biological reason that their *limbic system* is more developed than their *prefrontal cortex (PFC)*.

The limbic system, centrally located in our brain and one of the earliest brain regions to have evolved, registers and relays sensory information and processes emotions, including pleasure and pain. This *emotional brain* is fully functional at birth. It's a key survival mechanism for a newborn to tell us—usually loudly—when they are hungry, thirsty, or experiencing discomfort.

The most recently evolved part of our brain is the prefrontal cortex (PFC). The PFC, located just behind the forehead, is largely responsible for executive functions such as decision making, problem solving, judgment, impulse control, attention, concentration, and focus. It's commonly referred to as our *thinking brain*. The PFC is the last part of the brain to fully mature and be interconnected with other brain regions.

It's been said that, in terms of emotions, teenagers are driving a Ferrari equipped with Model T brakes. That image is pretty accurate; there is a huge performance gap between our teens' highly developed limbic system, the emotional brain center, and their still developing PFC, the center of rational thought.

This may be triggering an "Aha!" moment for you. You have probably seen many instances when your child's fully developed limbic system was off and running while the PFC was still trying to find its sneakers. At these times, our teens can be overreactive, volatile, and unpredictable, which can cause parents a good deal of distress.

But it's important to understand that these situations are as distressing for teenagers as they are for the adults around them, maybe even more so. It can be frightening to lose control over your emotions and not understand why. It can be terrifying to lash out at the very people you love and respect most. Teens often feel blindsided by the unpredictable and seemingly uncontrollable emotional avalanches they begin to experience on a regular basis. Some teens I've worked with have said it makes them feel like they are going crazy.

Sadly, most adolescents aren't aware that this is typical behavior driven by normal developmental processes associated with puberty and brain development. Therefore, it's important for parents to understand what is happening and reassure kids that their strong emotional reactions are perfectly normal and represent a short-term challenge, not a permanent character flaw.

CHAPTER 3

Individual Influences

Knowing what to expect and what is and isn't typical in development is important, but it only goes so far to help us understand what's going on. We can credit our uniqueness and individuality to the countless experiential, environmental, and situational factors we encounter throughout our lives.

SLEEP

I cannot overstate how sleep deprived our kids are today, nor can I overstate the negative impact this lack of sleep has on them both physically and mentally.

The National Sleep Foundation published a report in 2015 with the following recommendations:

Age	Hours of Sleep
Young adults (18 to 25)	7 to 9
Teens (14 to 17)	8 to 10
Children (6 to 13)	9 to 11

When I speak to groups of students, or work with them in a coaching capacity, I always ask them how much sleep they get each night. The majority say they sleep about 5 to 7 hours a night, which is consistent with national survey data. This means that most students are getting somewhere between 30 and 35 percent less sleep per night than they should be getting.

Many children are sleep deprived, including most disintegrating students.

As parents, we see the toll that lack of sleep takes on our kids. Emotionally, they are more volatile, irritable, aggressive, moody, and anxious. Physically, they are more likely to be injured while playing a sport, more likely to catch a cold or other virus, and are even more prone to rashes and acne. Sleep deprivation can contribute to poor nutritional choices, with teens opting for a quick carbohydrate and sugar fix rather than a more balanced meal. Fatigue impacts their activity level, which can lead to weight gain and other health-related issues.

Unfortunately for our students, there is a complete mismatch between the reality of their overscheduled

lives and the way their brains handle sleep. Just to com-
plicate things, nature plays a cruel trick on our teens by
making it harder for them to fall asleep at night. Right
around puberty, a shift in the human sleep cycle results
in a delay in the release of melatonin, a sleep-inducing
hormone produced by the brain. In younger children
and adults, melatonin is released around 9:00 p.m., but
in puberty the brain starts delaying the production
of melatonin until around 11:00 p.m. or later. When
your teen says, "I'm not tired" at midnight, they mean
it; they may be severely sleep deprived, but their brain
doesn't have that melatonin-induced sleepy feeling.*

Combining delayed melatonin release with other
modern-day sleep crushers is a recipe for disaster when
it comes to getting the beneficial rest teens (and parents) need. The body's *circadian (sleep/wake) cycle* is run
by the presence or absence of sunlight. Artificial light
that mimics natural sunlight sends our brains the signal that it's still daytime, not time for sleep, and delays
melatonin production even further. It is now known
that the blue light our screens emit is, to our brains,
indiscernible from sunlight, so the screens that many
of us take to bed with us to help us fall asleep are actually keeping us awake longer.

---

* One theory is that this shift in timing of the release of
melatonin is a residual adaptation from our earliest human
ancestors. Staggered sleep patterns would have meant group
members being alert to predators at different times.

Making matters even worse, evening is when many teens are doing their homework and studying. They are likely using a laptop, smartphone, or other device to access school websites and study materials (as well as to socialize with their friends). This screen exposure, oftentimes right up to the moment of (finally) falling asleep, degrades the quality of the sleep they do get.

Sleep-deprived teens aren't just emotional, prone to accidents, and more likely to get sick, they are also poorer learners (such a waste of that magnificent spongy brain!). Lack of sleep makes it harder for teens to maintain their focus, concentration, and attention. Some studies have shown a sleep-deprived student's performance can drop (temporarily) as much as two full grade levels.

Sleep is essential to learning new things, which requires forming memories that connect new information with previous learning. Guess when learning is consolidated, and memories formed? You got it, during sleep! When we deprive ourselves of adequate and healthy sleep, we deprive ourselves of the chance to integrate the day's new information and experiences and form lasting memories.

Many disintegrating students rely on late-night study sessions and last-minute cramming to prepare for tests, failing to realize that they are grasping wisps of information that may not be retrievable the next day and almost certainly will have drifted away by the end of the semester and the final exam. It's tough to convince students they are better off getting a good night's sleep and triaging the material right before a test than staying up all night studying. The most helpful way to explain it is to convince them that sleep is an essential step in the learning process and not a waste of study time. The idea that sleep will actually help them consolidate information can be a powerful realization for students.

Making sure that your disintegrating student gets enough sleep may be a challenge, but it is a battle worth fighting.

MINDSET

A *mindset* is a default way of thinking about something. We have many mindsets around many things—aging, stress, political ideology, and intelligence—just to name a few. Mindsets are like mental habits, once established they become automatic and can be difficult to break. But just like any physical habit, with awareness and effort, we can shift our mindsets.

In her book *Mindset: The New Psychology of Success*, Carol Dweck identifies two fundamental approaches to dealing with life's challenges, the *growth mindset* and the *fixed mindset*. (I highly recommend that parents, teachers, and coaches read her book for a deeper understanding of how mindset influences our behavior.) In terms of their ability to handle increased academic rigor, there is a big difference between students with a growth mindset and those with a fixed mindset. Many disintegrating students have the latter.

Students with a growth mindset do not believe their intelligence or abilities to be finite or to have an upper limit. These students welcome challenges and see their inevitable mistakes and setbacks not as failures but as opportunities to learn and grow. This makes them receptive to feedback and coaching, and open to new ways of doing things. Their spongy brains work over-time to learn, improve, and grow!

Students with a fixed mindset see their intellectual capacity as having a fixed upper limit. They don't view an increase in rigor as an opportunity to expand and grow their intellect because they don't consider that to be possible. They believe they can only be as smart as they are. So when they find work difficult, it clearly means they have reached the upper limit of their abilities. These students are likely to feel threatened by (and avoid) challenges, because situations that feel difficult or frustrating seem like red flags, warning them that they aren't smart enough to meet the high standards of their peers, their parents, and the educational system as a whole. Unfortunately, their spongy brains work overtime to protect their self-esteem, to the detriment of new learning.

It's my experience that disintegrating students with a fixed mindset often don't seek help when they encounter challenges or experience setbacks. Why?

Because when smart kids start getting bad grades, the assault on their self-esteem can be extremely stressful, especially if they feel that they are disappointing other people. Keep in mind that these students have always done well in the past, and a good bit of their self-concept and identity has always been wrapped up in being smart—even *the smartest.*

I'll give you an example, involving one of my daughters, that really surprised me. In her freshman year of high school, I noticed she seemed unusually tense about school. When I asked if things were okay or if she wanted to talk about it, she said she was fine, or gave me generalities like, "I'm just tired."

Eventually, I discovered that she was more stressed than I knew, and it was because she had struggled in one particular class and had received her first-ever *B* on a report card. She thought she had disappointed me—and would have to keep disappointing me—because she was no longer my *smart* daughter.

Now, to be perfectly honest, because her dad and I had always tried not to overly focus on our kids' grades, we were surprised to learn that she was so concerned, and that it was her first-ever *B*, and that she thought she had let us down. Certainly, neither of us saw a *B* in high school as a sign of failure, nor did we think it was anything to worry about. But she had been carrying this heavy load of self-recrimination and self-doubt around for months. She was her own judge, jury, and executioner over a thing we didn't even know was a thing!

This was a lesson to me about how deeply stressful and disorienting a child's academic struggles can be, and how my daughter's fixed mindset was impacting her.

When disintegrating students start to struggle academically, they will go to great lengths to maintain the well-kept secret that they need help. They will often reject well-intentioned offers of assistance, because in their mind any such assistance might expose weaknesses and vulnerabilities that they are desperately trying to hide. They tell themselves, "Smart people don't ask for help. Smart people figure it out for themselves. Asking for help is a sign of weakness and stupidity. Asking for help is embarrassing."

In some cases, these students will try to cover their academic struggles with *self-sabotage*, creating a decoy explanation for their declining performance, which then actually does contribute to future failures. They may stop doing homework, or "forget" to turn in assignments, stop studying for tests, or adopt a negative or dismissive attitude toward school. They may say they don't care, but they really do, a lot. Some students may genuinely believe that they don't care, but typically they know they're not being honest with themselves or others.

Unfortunately, when our brains recognize an incongruity between what we think and what we say, it manifests that difference in feelings of anxiety. The stress of living in an inauthentic manner—thinking one way and behaving another—often catches up to these students and causes even further disintegration. They feel like a fraud with their friends, teachers, and family. They think, "No one really knows how messed up and confused I am, and I need to do everything possible to keep them from finding out." When not addressed properly, this anxiety can spiral into more serious issues such as insomnia, test anxiety, panic attacks, depression, or, in extreme situations, suicidal thoughts.

Many disintegrating students feel like their situation is unique, that it is happening only to them. Of course: all the other students experiencing disintegration are going to great lengths to hide *their* struggles too! This isolation feeds the cycle of fear and self-recrimination that prevents our kids from seeking help when they need it.

INNER MONOLOGUE

Students most at risk of disintegration tend to experience or perceive pressure coming from everyone, everywhere, all the time. They worry about the expectations of family members (including siblings and grandparents), teachers, and friends. They especially worry about the expectations of the colleges they are interested in. They carry on an inner monologue, telling themselves that everyone expects great things from them, and the only way to succeed is to never, ever fail, to deliver 100 percent all the time, in everything. In a word, they become perfectionists.

Contrary to popular belief, a perfectionist is not a person who does everything perfectly. Quite the opposite! Perfectionists are constantly reaching for impossibly high personal standards with overly critical self-appraisal. To a perfectionist nothing is ever perfect, and if it isn't perfect it's garbage. Disintegrating students tend to view situations as either black or white. They tell themselves, "Either I get the highest grade on the test, or I've failed. If I don't make first string, I'm a scrub. If my friends don't love me, they hate me. If I can't keep a 4.0 GPA, I'm dumb, so why study at all?"

The inner monologue of a disintegrating student often defaults to negative explanations for events and outcomes—"I'm stupid, everyone is stupid, everything is stupid"—that can easily turn into a downward spiral of self-doubt and self-sabotage. When they direct that negativity outward it may appear that they are not taking responsibility for their own actions, but in reality, they are just trying to insulate themselves from the stress of additional judgment, real or imagined.

When a perfectionist encounters failure, as we all do at some point in our lives, the emotional mind can overwhelm the thinking mind, causing performance to decline even more. This stressful and threatening situation may immobilize a disintegrating student and make it impossible for them to accomplish anything.

PROCRASTINATION

With very few exceptions, humans prefer doing things we enjoy instead of things we don't enjoy, and procrastination lets us put off something we'd rather not do for as long as possible. If we can find something to do that we enjoy instead of something we don't enjoy, all the better. This easily explains why a student might put off doing homework and play a video game instead.

But there are other, more complicated physiological reasons that students procrastinate. In a study, participants were asked to think about themselves doing something right now and then asked to think about someone *else* doing something right now. Brain imaging showed that two different areas of the brain lit up depending on whether they were thinking of themselves or someone else doing the task.

The interesting thing is that when participants were asked to think about themselves doing something *in the future*, the part of the brain associated with *someone else* lit up. This helps to explain why procrastination feels so good. When we say, "I'll do it later," as far as our brains are concerned, we're outsourcing the task to a completely different person, and not to our future self. The obvious problem is that your future self is not a superhero who can easily handle the work you're putting off. It's just *you*, but more stressed out, with more stuff to do, and not feeling too happy about your past self's choices.

When students procrastinate until they are *forced* to do the thing they've been putting off, their bodies release adrenaline, a hormone that increases the rate of blood circulation, breathing, carbohydrate metabolism, and prepares muscles for exertion. The same *fight or flight* reaction that would help you confront a wild animal in the woods convinces your child that they work best under pressure, because they mistake the adrenaline rush for increased competency.

Of course, research into procrastination tells a different story. The adrenaline rush gives us an illusion of high performance, whether or not we do good work. While an individual may still produce something good after waiting until the last minute, they would almost always do better with more time.

Another reason people procrastinate is to avoid pain, which is one of the most basic human instincts. But why would a student procrastinate on a homework assignment? How much pain can be ascribed to that? Well, think about that homework assignment in the context of a disintegrating student. They're already finding their work challenging (which threatens their self-esteem), ambiguous (which requires seeking help), and frustrating (which is a challenge for anyone!). Their brains, instinctively trying to avoid pain, will often suggest another activity, one that will trigger the release of feel-good chemicals as a reward. "Wouldn't it be better," says the brain, "to play a video game instead, just for a little while, before you do that awful thing that makes you feel stupid and helpless?"

And then it's midnight, and they're out of time.

It's not uncommon for me to hear parents (and students themselves) use the word "lazy" to describe a disintegrating student who procrastinates. Most times they're using the word incorrectly. To be lazy is not to care. Students who don't complete assignments are lazy only if they truly don't care at all about learning or getting good grades. That's rarely the case with disintegrating students. Remember what they told us in their own words: "We care so much it's scary." A disintegrating student who engages in procrastination usually does care, quite a bit, about completing the task they are delaying, but their brain convinces them that it's okay to do it later instead of now.

As a college freshman, Lily learned how easy it is to procrastinate, and the problems it can cause.

> Lily was always a great student and took all the advanced and accelerated courses she could. She graduated high school with a 3.87 GPA and was accepted to a state college about two hours away from her home. "Excited" didn't even begin to describe how Lily felt as she headed off to school.
>
> Her college experience began early with sorority rush. After a fun but exhausting week, she excitedly accepted a bid from her

first-choice sorority. The friendships, the parties—college was going to be awesome!!

But then classes started. Lily had declared a Hospitality Management major because she had loved to throw parties since she was little and dreamed of a career running large events at fancy hotels. But none of her first semester courses had anything to do with event planning, just boring requirements and some "lame course" for incoming freshmen. Her sorority, on the other hand, really valued her event-planning skills. The dull, pointless homework took a back seat to what she really enjoyed.

Lily's parents became concerned early on. Lily kept telling them all about her social life, but she said very little about classes. When they asked about her grades, Lily usually said she didn't know yet.

That was partly true. The few test grades she did have were mostly *Cs* and few low *Bs*, but she had no idea how they would impact her final grades or whether she could bring them up, so she preferred not to think about it too much. She also didn't like to think about the classes she was missing, especially her Monday 8:00 a.m. class (after a weekend of partying) and her Friday classes (after Thursday night mixers).

Lily realized this pattern wasn't sustainable, and that her parents were going to freak when they saw her grades. She began to attend classes more regularly. She talked with her teachers and tried to study. She didn't give up her social life, but she did cut back a bit. Not surprising, the last four weeks of the semester were unbelievably stressful and overwhelming. Although she managed to pull two *B*s and two *C*s, she broke down in tears nearly every day from exhaustion and frustration.

When she came home for the winter break Lily fell apart. "I'm not smart enough for college! I can't do this. My roommate's a jerk, my teachers don't care, and it's just too hard!"

But it wasn't the work that was too hard for Lily. She was supersmart and more than capable of doing it. What was difficult for Lily was choosing the discomfort of doing the work over the pleasure of avoiding it.

MOTIVATION

The motivational drive to do well can be *intrinsic* (internally rewarding and originating within ourselves) or *extrinsic* (driven by external rewards such as praise, attention, money, or grades).

Ideally, the process of learning should be internally rewarding, and intrinsically motivated. Many of the most successful and satisfied adults describe themselves as life-long learners, driven by their personal experiences and curiosities to continually ask questions and discover new things. They have an appetite for learning which, when fed, they find very rewarding.

Learning in infancy and early childhood is largely characterized by intrinsic motivation. But we gradually become programmed by, and accustomed to, the external rewards offered in exchange for doing something, which gradually erodes intrinsic motivation. We get praised for being polite, we get check marks and stickers for good grades, and we get paid for doing chores. Although we like the rewards, the more we rely on extrinsic motivation to do something—*if* you do X, *then* you get Y—the less meaningful and enjoyable the task becomes. When students focus on, and work for, the external rewards associated with learning (e.g., grades, awards, praise, money) it actually decreases their enjoyment and derails their intrinsic motivation.

This paradox is backed up by lots of research that has demonstrated the harmful consequences of external incentives. Studies tell us that not only is working for external rewards less satisfying, but also that these incentives actually result in a decline in performance. External rewards put additional pressures on a task and misdirect focus away from the task in ways that are not beneficial. Many parents try giving bigger rewards, but the motivation is still not there.

This means that students who are predominantly extrinsically motivated present a challenge when the rewards are not working. The key is to help them find their way back to being intrinsically motivated to learn.

Let's say as a parent you have offered an incentive to your child to study. If your child studies for 30 minutes, you give them 30 minutes of screen time. They may put in the time studying to get the thing they want, but it is unlikely that they will get much out of the time they spend studying. More likely, they will spend 30 minutes learning very little in order to get you off their back. And what if 30 minutes of screen time does not motivate them even to pretend to study? Would an offer of 45 minutes of screen time be more effective? Probably not. If a student's motivation to learn is driven solely by extrinsic rewards, they are unlikely to do well in school. The key is to shift the motivation from extrinsic to intrinsic, and this may require some hard choices for parents and hard lessons for students.

As a parent in this situation, you have to let your child make their own choice—to do the work or not do the work—and experience the natural consequences that will result. This means you have to allow your child to fail on occasion.

My son, the oldest of my three children, became intrinsically motivated in high school. He was always a high achiever who didn't have to put much effort into his schoolwork, until he started to disintegrate during his sophomore year. When he reached his rigor tipping point, he started to miss homework assignments, saw his grades slide, and spent a disturbingly high number of hours playing video games.

My husband and I tried all the usual tricks to motivate him. But none of them worked. He did just enough to get by and get us off his back for a while.

This changed in his junior year, when he had a very good, but tough AP Calculus teacher. The first semester, my son's performance was straight out of his sophomore year playbook, which is to say, lackluster. When it came time to register for senior courses, he assumed he'd go on to the next level of AP Calculus but was quickly disabused of that idea. His calculus teacher refused to sign the course request, saying (rightly) that my son had not demonstrated a willingness to do AP-level work.

Well, talk about igniting a fire in a kid! Righteously indignant, my son was determined to prove to his teacher (and, more importantly, to himself) that he could do AP-level math. For the remainder of his junior year he received top marks on every quiz and test. He received approval for the senior-level AP course, and continued to excel. He was given extra responsibilities in the math department and was recognized for his achievements at graduation. But along the way, something interesting had happened. My son continued his curve-busting math achievements throughout college, but he was no longer motivated by the external pressure of rewards, recognitions, or proving himself to someone else. He excelled because the learning process itself had become meaningful to him and motivated him to do his best.

SOCIAL PEER PRESSURE

Adolescents care deeply about what other adolescents think about them. Peer acceptance becomes particularly important in the middle school and high school years. It's a fairly safe bet that if a teen has done something out of character, it's because they succumbed to peer pressure.

Why do their peers matter so much to them? Much of it is instinctual; the human brain has evolved for social connection. From the time of the caveman, belonging to a *tribe* has provided safety and resources that enhanced a tribe member's chances for survival, and tribe members with strong social instincts were more likely to reproduce and pass those traits along. Social connections are so important to us that brain imaging shows that social slights, exclusions, and isolation activate the same brain areas as physical pain. Because our brain treats being left out as painful, we are driven to behave in ways that help us be accepted by the group in order to avoid pain.

When friends pressure each other to take an action

that they might not otherwise take, because "everyone's doing it," the emotional brain sees the threat of being left out of the group as very real and highly motivating. Even though an adolescent's prefrontal cortex (PFC) will try to exert judgment and impulse control, while in this anxious state the thinking brain often loses.

Here's an example to illustrate how this plays out in real life and how we can find ways to mediate this temporary developmental hiccup. An eighth-grade girl joins her friends for typical Saturday night sleepover. But this time one of her friends shares that she has a water bottle filled with vodka that she got from her parents' liquor cabinet. What does she do? If you asked her prior to the sleepover if she would drink alcohol, she would genuinely and emphatically deny that she would, yet when faced with the pressure of her friends' urging, and the availability of the alcohol, and a brain bathed in the fear of being left out, she likely caves to the pressure (against her thinking brain's better judgment) and drinks the vodka. This is not surprising considering that when we survey adolescents about what they would do in a risky situation such as being offered alcohol or drugs, they usually tell us they would just refuse to join in, end of story, no big deal. What they don't factor in is the potential pushback from their friends, which triggers their brains' instinctual fear of exclusion, increasing the likelihood they will succumb to peer pressure against their better judgment.

Studies have shown that informational campaigns for things such as alcohol and drugs, safe sex, and internet safety are very effective in delivering information to children, but very ineffective at changing behavior. Kids know this stuff. They understand the implications, risks, and potential consequences. But it turns out that knowing about it is not enough. The fact that the PFC is not fully developed in adolescents means their thinking brain rarely stands a chance in a contest with their emotional brain.

One way to mediate this hiccup is with some proactive planning. Parents can talk through various scenarios with their kids and have them consider and rehearse their responses. For example, my advice to my own children has been to fake feeling sick so they can head to a bathroom to escape stressful pressure long enough to think through a plan of action, call a parent, or otherwise bypass the situation. In other words, give their thinking brain a chance to get back online. It's also helpful for kids to come up with and memorize things they could say in response to a friend pressuring them. Then, when under pressure the thinking brain doesn't need to think through what to do but instead relies on a well-learned set of responses that are easily accessible.

ACADEMIC PEER PRESSURE

Supersmart students tend to socialize with each other based on class assignments, course selections, and shared interests. Having the best and brightest kids as friends can have a very positive influence on students, when everyone encourages each other to be the best version of themselves.

But problems arise when academically talented students stop being supportive of each other and become competitive instead. This can lead to students being pressured into taking courses that are too difficult for them or overloading their schedule with more courses and extracurricular activities than they can handle. Sometimes this pressure comes directly from other students: "You need this AP! Colleges want you to have this course. We're all taking it. You don't want to be on-level; you'll be so bored." Other times the pressure will be internal, with students feeling like they have to maintain a difficult schedule to prove to themselves that they are the smartest kid in the class. Sometimes, sadly, parents exert unhealthy academic pressure on their children as well.

Adolescents are in constant comparison mode, always looking at what other adolescents are doing, saying, wearing, and what grades or recognitions they are receiving. As parents, we may do the same thing, often without even realizing it. Have you ever asked something like: "How did everyone else do on the test?" This seems like a perfectly reasonable question, but rather than asking them to compare their performance to their own skills or past experiences, we're asking them to measure their results in comparison to that of other students. It really doesn't matter how the other kids did. What matters is what our child has learned. (And if they didn't get a perfect score, now would be a good time for them to employ a growth mindset and view their mistakes not as failures but as opportunities to learn and grow.)

College prep can be an extremely stressful time for students and parents. Getting into college today is nothing like it used to be. When I graduated high school in the early 1980s, I took the ACT, filled out (by hand) an application to my big in-state university, wrote a check for $25, and mailed it in. My recollection is that I had very few conversations with my parents about college beyond making payments and moving me into my dorm. (And my occasional threat not to go to college at all, which was a very effective emotional trigger whenever I needed to derail my mom's focus from something else.)

In today's world, students and parents start talking about college prep as early as middle school. What's changed? The short answer is that our post–high school expectations and options have narrowed over the past few decades. While many of my classmates went to college after graduation, probably just as many went straight into the workforce or joined the military. These were all valid and reasonable options and there wasn't a lot of judgment or concern over the paths chosen.

There is a general assumption today that to be successful you must go to college and get a degree, which has become as expected and required as the high school diploma once was. The pressure on students to apply to, and be accepted by, reputable colleges and universities is intense.

As students are run through the college application wringer, the pressure and uncertainty turn many of them into walking curriculum vitae, eyeing each other warily and comparing stats. Their grades, nominations and awards, class rank, and college aspirations all become fair game for comparison and judgment, fueling students' deepest fears about their relative worth and potential.

How does all this impact our children? It's stressful, unreasonably stressful. Many students feel as though their entire future is at stake as they navigate the college prep experience. And, perhaps even more stressful for them is the feeling that their reputation is at stake. If they've always been recognized as a really smart kid and a high-achieving student then they should be accepted to a good university, right? Yet with record numbers of applicants to colleges and universities, it's not enough anymore to be a high-achieving, super-smart student. Students with grade point averages above 4.0 and laundry lists of extracurricular activities are rejected by many selective schools in astonishing and disturbing numbers, not because they wouldn't be successful there, but because of the sheer volume of applicants.

The academic pressures placed on supersmart kids by themselves, their parents, and their peers are enormous, and can cause even the smartest of them to fall apart.

CHAPTER 4

Cultural Influences

ADULTING

I'M FASCINATED by the word "adulting," which is used by teenagers and young adults—often ironically or derisively—to describe what they do when they act like adults. Prior generations stopped being children and became adults in their late teens or early twenties, but Millennials (born 1981–96) and post-Millennials (born 1997–present) have found a way to shift in and out of adulthood simply by "adulting" whenever they find it necessary, or convenient, to do so.

Some may say that Millennials and post-Millennials (also known as Gen-Z or I-Gen) choose adulting over *adulthood* because there's something fundamentally wrong with them that makes them unable or unwilling to accept all the responsibilities that come with being an actual adult. People insist that there is something particularly unusual about these teens and young adults that makes them unlike any prior generation and unable to handle adulthood.

Personally, I'm not satisfied with this argument. First, because I think it's based on a false premise: that Millennials and post-Millennials can't handle being an adult. Second, because the argument fails to explain how an entire generation of children, from a wide variety of backgrounds, have chosen to delay their entry into the adult world and have come to see adulthood as an activity instead of an identity, a frame of mind rather than a reflection of their chronological age with its accompanying personal and social responsibilities.

There's no question that Millennials and post-Millennials, raised by the youngest Baby Boomers (born in the early 1950s) and the Gen-Xers (born 1965–80), have their own brand of living, working, and socializing, which is dramatically different from the generations that preceded them. Adulting appears to be part of that brand, and there are a number of factors that explain why.

Part of the reason lies in physiology. Recall from Chapter 2 that current research shows adolescent changes in the brain are not complete until far later than previously thought, and that neuropsychologists now know that, with regard to brain maturity, adolescence doesn't end until around age 25 in many people. Prior generations felt compelled to "grow up" around the age of 18. Perhaps today's youth has simply figured out that most 18-year-olds are not yet full-fledged adults.

Some of the differences between today's youth

and prior generations are the result of technological changes. From the introduction of the iPhone in 2007 to the growth of omnipresent social media (Facebook launched in 2004, Twitter in 2006, Instagram in 2010, and Snapchat in 2012), today's young people are able to connect and share information in ways that Baby Boomers and Gen-Xers couldn't even dream of when they were growing up. This hyperconnectivity, and the social pressures it creates, has had a profound impact on Millennials and post-Millennials.

But the most important differences between today's students and prior generations are driven by fundamental changes in the norms of parenting that took place in the late twentieth century and changes in our education system that occurred in the early twenty-first century, both of which contributed to creating an entire generation of anxious, insecure, stressed-out kids.

THE VIRTUAL WORLD

Through their smartphones students are now connected to each other 24/7, and to everyone else on the planet. They all know what everyone else is doing, when they're doing it, and who they're doing it with. They know when a close friend has been slighted, insulted, or hurt. They get slighted, insulted, and hurt themselves. Adolescents are spending less time face-to-face with friends and more time remotely connected. In-person conversations have been replaced by group chats.

Clearly there are some advantages to this. Adolescents know more people and can become "friends" much more easily without the need for direct, in-person contact, and the attendant risk of rejection that comes with it.

The disadvantage is that even though our teens are highly connected and have hundreds, maybe thousands of virtual friends, they are reporting unprecedented levels of loneliness. And we may joke about FOMO, or "Fear of Missing Out," but teens who disconnect or disengage from their peers in the virtual world run the very real risk of social isolation in the real world.

Remote relationships are problematic. Our instinctual drive to belong to a group and connect with others has remained fundamentally unchanged since our ancestors carried clubs and battled saber-toothed tigers. Fearing isolation, we developed a sensitivity to subtle cues from others in their vocalizations, facial expressions, gestures, and body language. When we strip our interactions of these fundamental building blocks of social interaction and connection, we are left with something that our brain doesn't fully recognize as *connection*. It feels empty, inauthentic and devoid of meaning. And that's how teens will often describe their relationships.

In addition to the lack of meaningful connection, teens know that almost everything in their virtual world is crafted and staged. They know this because they do it themselves. There are unwritten rules about how to take flattering photos, how to comment, what to comment, when to comment, and even how to use (or avoid) punctuation. There is a right and a wrong way to present your virtual self, which is almost always different from your actual self.

If everyone is doing it, and everyone knows everyone is doing it, why is it a problem? Because a true connection with another person requires revealing our authentic selves. In other words, we aren't putting on airs or trying to impress, but we are more real and vulnerable and can truly be seen by the other person for who we really are. This is what drives social connection: to be seen, heard, understood, and accepted by another on a profoundly personal level.

Unfortunately, this is not what teens are experiencing through their virtual connections. Virtual relationships have evolved into a specialized social experience that serves a purpose but cannot fill our profoundly important need for social connection. This translates into a highly connected, but acutely lonely generation.

CHANGING NORMS OF PARENTING

You may remember the heartbreaking case of Adam Walsh, a six-year-old boy who, in July 1981, went missing in Florida while shopping with his mother. He was later discovered to have been abducted and murdered. His father, John Walsh, went on to start the *America's Most Wanted* television program and became an influential political activist responsible for the creation of agencies and enactment of legislation aimed at protecting children. What's significant about this incident is that it unleashed a domino effect of consequences that ranged from national public policy to new parenting norms. Photos and bios of missing children were placed on milk cartons (*Have You Seen Me?*) and stores implemented Code Adam alerts (a predecessor to today's Amber Alert) to notify shoppers and employees of a missing child. The National Center for Missing and Exploited Children was created.

The abduction and murder of Adam Walsh, and the events that followed it, dramatically impacted the way late-Boomer and Gen-X parents raised their children. Even though it was not supported by actual statistics, parents came to believe that the world is a fundamentally dangerous place and that children must be protected and closely monitored at all times. The cultural message that pervaded society was that good parents never lose sight of their kids.

Late-Boomer and Gen-X parents also came of age when women were demanding and making progress toward equal opportunities in the work force. The tradeoff was more children home alone. Widely referred to as *latchkey kids*, children of working parents would come home to an empty house and let themselves in.

But with the emphasis on safety at all times, they were likely required to call a parent at work by a certain time to let them know they were home, safe and secure, and would stay there.

Of course, this contrasted greatly with the childhoods of their parents, whose experience probably had been to come home from school to a waiting parent, most often their mother, who'd give them a snack and then let them go off and roam the neighborhood alone or with friends, usually returning home just in time for dinner. Keenly aware of the discrepancies between their own childhood freedoms and their children's lack of freedom, these parents came up with a compromise: the *playdate*.

Playdates became the norm for young Millennials and post-Millennials as their parents, again usually moms, became social planners for their children starting in infancy and continuing, in at least some form, well into adolescence. The playdate both solved a problem and created new ones. Children had opportunities to socialize with same-age playmates, but not in an unstructured, unsupervised manner. Socialization took place under the watchful eyes of parents ready to spring into action at the first sign of distress, danger, or conflict, thus depriving children of the opportunities to learn and develop valuable interpersonal skills on their own. As a result, children came to rely on their parents to resolve conflicts and intervene on their behalf. Over time, this reliance extended to many other areas of their lives as well.

Another cultural shift that occurred during the 1980s was that society came to view a child's self-esteem as being a key driver and determinant of their success. The idea was that if children feel good about themselves, they will succeed in life. If we told them they were special, they would be. In an effort to preserve and increase the self-esteem of our children, we adopted an approach to teaching, coaching, and parenting in which every child was recognized, rewarded, and praised for everything they did. Thus, the *Everyone Gets A Trophy* movement was born.

Why did this well-intentioned "everyone is awesome" approach to raising children not work as well as everyone thought it would? Simply put, kids figured out that just showing up is not much of an achievement and coming in last is nothing to celebrate. Psychologically speaking, giving kids rewards that weren't even remotely connected to their effort and performance resulted in *cognitive dissonance*, the mental discomfort experienced by a person holding two contradictory ideas, beliefs or values at the same time. It didn't make children feel more secure, confident, capable, and happy. It had the exact opposite effect and made them feel insecure, uncertain, helpless, and unhappy. It also heavily contributes to the shifts in mindset we see in children as they go through school—from a helpful growth mindset to the more limiting fixed mindset.

All of these factors—overprotective parenting, latchkey kids, *Everyone Gets A Trophy*—have contributed to the creation of a psychologically fragile generation of young adults with fixed mindsets. Young adults are the largest and fastest-growing group of people being diagnosed with anxiety disorders. College and university counseling centers are overwhelmed. The number of students seeking mental health support has increased, as has the scope and severity of need. Many students are presenting themselves to counseling centers in crisis, and the triggers are often things like a bad grade or a roommate issue. Safe spaces are popping up around college campuses for students who need to decompress and engage in calming activities.

EDUCATION POLICY

Changes in our education system over the last two decades have arguably been the most significant contributor to the rise in the number of disintegrating students. Many of the serious problems we face today are the indirect result of the No Child Left Behind Act of 2001 (NCLB).

NCLB became public policy during the George W. Bush administration and was in effect from 2002–2015. It was designed to improve education by holding schools accountable for kids' learning and achievement, and penalizing schools that didn't show positive results and improvement. The law was well-intentioned, but highly flawed in not anticipating the unintended consequences that came from incentivizing achievement, and punishing lack of achievement, through funding.

To remain in good standing, and more importantly to continue to receive funding, schools had to focus on gathering and reporting student data at the expense of traditional teaching. School became less about learning and more about testing, testing, and more testing. Teachers' job performance became tied to their students' test scores, pressuring them to "teach to the test." Education shifted from being student centered to institution centered, and our kids became data points.

NCLB's myopic focus on quantitative measurements of school and student outcomes shifted responsibility for education policy away from child-development experts, psychologists, and educators and toward business executives and politicians. In order to meet federal mandates for funding, schools scrambled to implement policies designed to enhance their performance scores, but not necessarily to improve student learning. It became common practice to give worksheets to kindergarteners, assign homework to first-graders, eliminate recess, cut programs for art and music, and encourage enrollment in advanced classes.

The mismatch between policies enacted under NCLB and appropriate developmental standards for students has proved catastrophic for our children. For young children, school should be a place for exploring and developing social skills through structured play, exposure, and incidental learning. Instead we are forcing developmentally inappropriate rigor down their throats. It should be the rare case that a first or second-grader hates school, but we are now seeing more and more of our youngest elementary kids with symptoms consistent with anxiety, depression, and school phobia. Schools are no longer interested in the unique talents, gifts, and developmental trajectory of individual students. Instead all students are expected to be above (well above) average and to achieve in the narrowly prescribed vacuum that is education today.

Students who do not perform *well above average* on standardized tests feel intense pressure from their peers, teachers, and parents to meet what feels like (and is, for them) a set of unreasonable standards. Many of them are told, and come to believe, that the problem lies with them, not the educational system, and they're just not trying hard enough. When these students repeatedly fail to meet arbitrary standards, they eventually give up. They hate school, they hate learning, and they can't wait for it to be over with.

It's not just students who are being harmed; teachers are being harmed as well. Teaching has become so tied to standardized methodology that it leaves little room for creativity based on teachers' understanding of, and relationships with, their students. Many excellent, seasoned teachers have left the field in frustration, and many teachers have stayed in teaching long after their frustration has turned to apathy. Teaching has become a substantially different endeavor from what it was prior to NCLB, and talented teachers are burning out under the constant pressure to meet new standards imposed on them, teach to the standardized test, and report results, without regard for students' overall well-being or actual learning.

The amount of testing is harmful to all students. Consider how you would feel in a job where every few months your boss tells you he's giving you a test to determine your worth as an employee, and the results will be used to determine your future opportunities within the company. When you take the tests, you realize that some of the questions have nothing to do with your job, and none of it adequately reflects the knowledge and skills that you bring to the table. This must be how students feel as they are subjected to endless testing.

One of the ways students react to the pressure of this perpetual testing is to become anxious and overly cautious. Children as young as first grade are experiencing signs of anxiety such as stomachaches, headaches, and school avoidance. These early grades should be a time when kids love to learn, but they're learning to fear judgment instead. Physical and emotional complaints are increasingly common among older students, too.

The importance assigned to testing in our schools has contributed to a significant increase in test anxiety, a physiological arousal that occurs before and/

or during a testing situation. There have always been kids who don't test well for various reasons, but what is happening now goes far beyond historical norms. Test anxiety is showing up far more frequently than in the past and affects a broader demographic of students.

Test anxiety today is being cultivated quite early, in the elementary years. I've heard heartbreaking accounts of students becoming ill or losing sleep because a teacher said that they must do well on a test to be promoted to the next grade. Teachers never intend to sabotage their students, but the stakes are high for them as well, with their compensation, and potentially their job, contingent on reporting high student test scores. Under this pressure, teachers' anxieties and frustrations may unintentionally leak out to their students. These moments of stress create a ripple effect as the word quickly spreads among the students: "This test is do or die!"

Parents who get wind of this will reassure their child that there's no risk of failing the grade, so they shouldn't worry about the test. However, children may be more likely to believe what the teacher has said over a parent's attempt to reassure them.

To perform well on a test, students must be able to:

- Read and understand the questions.

- Search long-term memory for the relevant information.

- Consider multiple options, narrow choices, and decide on the best possible answer.

- Accurately record the responses.

- Complete the process within a time limit.

Students who experience test anxiety aren't able to do these things effectively because their emotional brain overpowers their thinking brain.

A typical scenario for a student with test anxiety involves arriving to class, nervous but ready to take the test, only to face an onslaught of fearmongering and freaking out from their classmates. "I studied for six hours last night! I totally don't understand [insert concept here]! I heard the last class said this test is impossible! There's no way I'm going to pass!" Naturally, an anxious student will start second-guessing their own readiness, losing any confidence they may have had. The emotional brain takes notice of this sudden change and sounds the alarm, triggering a massive release of adrenaline. The fight or flight stress response causes a significant decline in the student's ability to think clearly, with the expected negative impact on their test performance.

Once a student experiences test anxiety, particularly if the resulting grade is below what they anticipated, they may become caught in a self-perpetuating cycle.

The memory of anxiety triggers the same worries about the next test. Negative self-talk takes over and results in poor preparation. The student feels even less confident, causing even higher anxiety when they take the next test, and so on. In an attempt to manage the stress, some students may eventually begin to sabotage themselves by opting not to study at all, justifying it by saying: "What difference is it going to make? I'm just going to blow it anyway."

CHAPTER 5

Parental Influences

GOOD INTENTIONS

AS I LOOK BACK at my twenty-plus years as a mom, I literally cringe at some of the mistakes I made raising my kids. There were times, particularly as a new mom with my firstborn, that I was way too overprotective of and hyperfocused on my children. Yet, I now realize that there were other times when I was completely oblivious to the gravity of issues impacting them.

I've had many days when I've felt like a total rock-star mom and other days when I felt deflated, defeated, and completely inadequate. I prefer the former (just sayin'), but I actually don't regret the latter. In a funny way, I'm as proud of the cringe-worthy moments as I am of the good ones. If you've had your own parenting ups and downs, you should be proud too. Here's why:

There are many parenting books, but not a single manual that works for everyone all the time. There is no parenting gold standard, just a lot of well-intentioned parents loving their children and trying very hard to

60

help them grow and thrive. I truly believe that any parent who cares enough to lie awake thinking about whether they're getting it right, who's willing to try new things and take risks, and who is able to endure the occasional parenting failure, is a freaking awesome parent! If this describes you, take a bow. You deserve some appreciation.

As parents, we have a great deal at stake when it comes to our children. We are programmed by evolution and biology to protect them. While the means by which we protect them has changed over many thousands of years, the drive to give our children what they need is just as emotionally intense as it ever was, and it often leads us to do things that are amazing, unbelievable, unexpected, and borderline superhuman. It can also lead us to make occasional mistakes.

Parents tend to have somewhat fragile egos when it comes to their parenting styles. It's very easy to become defensive when we feel we are falling short in our parenting responsibilities or that we are being judged by others on how we raise our kids. I've certainly been there myself. What helped me to become less sensitive to these perceived critiques was talking openly and honestly with other parents about the things we have done right *and* the mistakes we have made. Rather than cherry picking the best moments and sharing only my parenting wins, I found that being vulnerable and honest about my own parenting struggles opened the door to a safe space filled with empathy and reciprocity from others.

One commonality I noticed between myself and other parents was how often we thought we were doing the right thing but saw in hindsight that our actions had not worked as well as we intended. That's what this chapter is really about: how good intentions can go bad when it comes to parenting.

Here's just a partial list of good intentions that *may* result in unintended negative consequences:

- Praising
- Protecting, shielding, and sheltering
- Alleviating stress
- Helping and supporting
- Indulging
- Prioritizing

PRAISING

Telling children that they are awesome is a sweet, thoughtful, and supportive thing to do, within reason. Everyone likes to be recognized for their hard work and their achievements, and we usually feel good when someone says something good about us. It's natural to think that if a little praise is good, a lot of praise must always be better. What many people don't realize is that unearned, overused, or inappropriate praise can have a negative impact on students and their performance.

One problem with receiving unearned, overused, or inappropriate praise is both simple and obvious. The person receiving the praise comes to believe that they do everything perfectly and have no need to change or improve. This can lead to overconfidence and conceit, stifling a student's desire to learn and grow.

Another problem is less obvious, and a bit more complicated. Earned praise develops and validates an accurate self-image. Our self-esteem is the result of a delicate relationship between our intentions and effort, and the response we get from others. When children work hard for something, praise is a positive reinforcement for the work and the outcome. They feel justifiably proud of themselves, and more confident in their ability to take on challenges and succeed. This kind of accurate and appropriate praise is crucial to the development of a healthy and *congruent self-concept*, meaning that the way we see ourselves is consistent with the way others see us and the way we truly are.

However, unearned, overused, or inaccurate praise creates an internal conflict based on the difference between what a person is being told and what they know (or believe) to be true: "My parents say I'm brilliant, but that can't be right because I'm really struggling in my math class."

Over time, this internal conflict can create anxiety

in our children, even if they're not consciously aware of it. In an effort to reduce this anxiety, it is common for kids to shift the internal conflict to an external source. When someone is told repeatedly that they are awesome in every way, they find it hard to accept responsibility when they do something that very clearly is *not* awesome. Rather than acknowledge their lack of awesomeness, they will look for someone or something else to blame for the problems they are having.

I once had an experience that illustrates the problems that can result from unearned, overused, or inappropriate praise. A student in one of my college classes—I'll call her Angela—had turned in a paper and received a lower grade than she expected. I provided her with quite a bit of specific feedback explaining the reasons she lost points, not least of which was a complete disregard for the actual assignment. I had asked for 2–4 pages, but she gave me more than eight rambling pages with no clear thesis, uneven structure, poor mechanics, and bad grammar.

I vividly recall Angela calling me while I was shopping one afternoon. She was livid! She told me in no uncertain terms that she was a great writer—her teachers had always told her so—and she had written a great paper. I gave her the justification for her grade (as best as I could while standing in the middle of Costco), but she would not be appeased. She was convinced that she was a great student who had written a near-perfect paper, and that I had not graded her paper correctly or fairly.

Angela held a grudge for the remainder of the semester, sitting in lectures with her arms firmly crossed, giving me the stink eye. She often shared things in class that reflected her sense that everyone was out to get her, that everyone was wrong about everything, and that everyone else was just plain stupid (which, of course, they weren't). Clearly, Angela had an unrealistically high opinion of her own abilities, and an internal conflict between what she had been told about her abilities and her actual performance. She attempted to resolve that conflict by blaming me and everyone else around her for her own shortcomings.

Of course, this does not mean that you should stop praising your children and start criticizing them instead. Praise is always preferable to criticism. The key takeaway is simply that praise should be given when warranted, not lavished for no reason.

What to do

How do we avoid turning praise into a negative? Research by Carol Dweck and others has shown that one of the keys to making praise effective is to focus on the *effort* (e.g., studying, practice, rehearsal) more than the *gift* (e.g., intellect, athleticism, talent). For example, parents and teachers often tell children how smart they are when they get high marks on a test. These compliments fall short because they aren't focused on the effort. If a student is smart when they get a good grade, are they *not* smart when they get a bad grade? Of course not. A bad grade is more likely caused by a lack of preparation than by an intellectual shortcoming. Praising the effort of studying is far more effective than praising the result of getting a good grade.

Shifting the focus of the praise away from what is *not* within the child's control (inborn gifts and talents) toward what *is* within their control (how hard they try) will foster a growth mindset in which new learning is met with interest, feedback becomes a welcomed part of improvement, and challenges are seen as fun and exciting rather than frustrating and threatening.

PROTECTING, SHIELDING, AND SHELTERING

How many of us have emailed a teacher, a coach, a school administrator or another child's parent in defense of an injustice, real or perceived, that was directed at our child? Not me! (Totally me. Probably you, too.) When I think my child is in danger or has been treated unfairly, my inner "mama bear" comes out of hibernation with a natural impulse to protect them, to right the wrong, and to hold someone accountable.

But being too involved in your child's activities or casting too wide a protective net can have the unintended consequence of undermining the development of your child's healthy self-concept and sense of efficacy in the world.

There are times when coming to the aid and defense of your child is unquestionably justified and necessary, and doing so will enhance your child's sense of safety and security. But coming to your child's defense every time something goes wrong in their life creates a sense of entitlement in them. They may come to believe that they are always right and everyone else is always wrong. It is so much more valuable to teach them when and how to stand up for themselves and solve their own problems. You will be giving them the gift of independence by helping them to develop the social skills they need to take care of themselves in the real world.

What to do

A good rule of thumb here is that if your child is not in immediate danger, hit the pause button and give them a chance to work things out for themselves. This might not be easy! If you have strong feelings about the situation, it's even more important to take the time to calm down and decide whether to intervene. This may involve sleeping on it, talking it out with a trusted friend or family member, venting your concerns in writing (preferably in a private journal or an email that you *won't* send), or just blowing off steam by taking a walk or exercising.

Once your cooler head prevails, *then* decide how to respond. If it's a situation your child can or should respond to on their own, with your support and guidance but without your direct involvement, let them. If it would be appropriate for you and your child to respond together or in coordination, try to let your child take the lead. If you've determined that a unilateral parent response is warranted, clarify your thoughts on what the perceived issue is, why it's a problem, and be clear on what you want or need to happen.

Our children watch us closely and take cues from adults on how to handle their own anger and frustration, so we should always try to model effective conflict resolution skills. Complaining about something without proposing a reasonable solution serves no purpose. In other words, always try to propose a solution to fix the problem you see, don't just complain about it and hope something gets done. It's perfectly appropriate to share your feelings of frustration, concern, or disappointment in communications with other people, but it never helps to be disrespectful, threatening, or rude. Such behavior is counterproductive and sets a bad example for our children.

ALLEVIATING STRESS

In addition to protecting our kids from the slights and injustices they encounter (real or perceived), parents often try hard to reduce their stress. We do this by removing obstacles and protecting them from outside stressors in an effort to prevent them from becoming overburdened or upset. The thought is that stress is a bad thing, so the elimination of stress must be a good thing, and the elimination of all stress must therefore be a great thing.

But stress is natural, designed to help you survive, and it can be very helpful when properly managed. If your life is in danger, your brain's fight or flight response will kick in and provide you with as much energy as possible to protect yourself, either by fighting back or by running away. During your body's stress response hormones such as cortisol, adrenaline, and epinephrine are released to give you a burst of energy, your liver dumps sugar and fat into your bloodstream, nonessential systems such as digestion and the immune system slow down, and smaller blood vessels constrict to limit blood loss in case you are injured.

The bad news is that while your body's stress response is exquisitely designed to protect you, it is meant to be engaged in short-term emergencies only. If your fight or flight stress response is continually engaging in response to the daily hassles you experience, then it can be harmful to you. Chronically high levels of cortisol, suppressed immune functioning, and chronically constricted blood vessels all contribute to the development of cardiovascular disease, metabolic disorders, and other diseases.

What to do

The good news is that just as we can use our body's stress response to fend off a mountain lion attack or to run away from danger, we can use our body's stress response to improve our performance in school and in life. The key is to view the thing causing our stress not as a threat, but as a challenge—something that elicits interest and excitement. This thinking results in a slight alteration in the physiology of stress, enough to make our body's response helpful in a non-life-threatening challenge and not detrimental to our health. When we view a stressor as a challenge and think of our body's physical response as giving us the energy to meet the challenge and perform at our best, we feel energized and confident.

This is the difference between performing well under pressure and choking. If you are taking a high-stakes test, you want a challenge-oriented stress response to be able to do your best. This can be achieved by altering your thoughts about the stress. Are your thoughts about failing, how hard it's going to be, or other negative (threatening) outcomes? Then expect to choke (or at least underperform). But when you reframe your thoughts to acknowledge the importance and challenge of the test as the source of your stress, you can choose to feel energized and engaged, which will fundamentally change how you perform—for the better! The key, therefore, is not to eliminate all stress but to learn how to use stress to your advantage.

HELPING AND SUPPORTING

Everyone needs help now and then. Humans are a social animal and we depend on each other for our very survival. Newborns depend on their parents for everything, but as children grow, they learn to do more and more for themselves. But regardless of how self-sufficient we become, we all feel more secure when we know that someone has our back.

There's nothing wrong with helping your adolescent children, and occasionally coming to their rescue as they learn to manage the responsibilities of life. Sometimes it really is necessary. But parents who are more comfortable being in control and are attuned to their children's stress are often tempted to provide help even when their kids neither need nor want it. Such unneeded and unwanted help can be detrimental to a child's development, depriving them of the opportunity to build the skills and confidence they need.

How many times has something like this happened in your house?

You: "Hey, please empty the dishwasher after dinner."

Child: "I can't. I have homework to do and
I'm way behind! I'm really stressed
right now." (For added emphasis,
they start to give off that unmistak-
able vibe of fraying at the edges;
clearly, one more word from us will
be their undoing!)

So what do we do? All too often, we cave and empty
the dishwasher ourselves, then we ask what else we can
do to help them out. We totally avoid the meltdown or
fight or whatever fresh hell is sure to come our way,
and we make an exception that lowers the bar for our
child's responsibilities within the family.

I have most definitely struggled with this issue. I
know my kids have a lot on their plates, and I don't
want to overburden them unnecessarily. But there's
a difference between being compassionate and being
played like a fiddle. We do our children a disservice
when we don't expect them to perform age-appropriate
chores and activities on a regular and consistent basis.
Beware, also, of the lure of your own competency. Yes,
it's often faster (and easier) to do things yourself to
avoid drama and keep everything running smoothly,
but if you always rely on your own competency you
prevent your kids from developing their own.

While our kids may be relieved and grateful in the
short term for being let off the hook, in the long term
if we bail them out on a regular basis, we run the risk

of sowing doubt in their minds about their own capabilities. In other words, if we don't expect very much
from our children, the subtle message we send is that
we don't think they can handle it. A steady diet of this
kind of thinking, even at an unconscious level, tends to
undermine feelings of autonomy, control, and efficacy,
and it ultimately negatively impacts their self-concept.

And when we go overboard, when we help our children *too* much, they come to accept that we will do
everything for them and expect that we'll bail them out
whenever they screw up. Have an issue with a teacher, a
coach, or a grade? Parent sends an email. Need to make
a doctor's appointment? Parent makes the call. Forgot
lunch? Mom cancels her lunch to bring yours. Left your
trumpet under your bed? Dad cancels a meeting to get
it for you. As parents we want to help our children, but
we do them a real disservice by doing everything for
them or coming to their rescue too quickly and too
often, and not occasionally letting them suffer the consequences of their actions, or inaction.

What to do

If you're doing everything for your child without being
asked, stop doing it. And if you're doing everything
for your child because you *are* being asked, stop doing
that too. Step back and let them take more responsibility for age-appropriate things they are capable of
doing themselves. They will appreciate being treated

like the adult they are in the process of becoming. If your adolescent or young-adult child is asking, or expecting, you to do almost everything for them, it's probably time for a little reality therapy. The reality is that you cannot (and absolutely should not) be doing so much for your teen. The real world will demand they know how to take care of their basic needs and responsibilities. Our job is to teach them how and help them learn to help themselves.

Have you ever tried to schedule an appointment for a high school student? Good grief! I have. It's not easy and it's certainly not fun. I remember trying to make appointments for my older daughter, and she'd give me all kinds of parameters: "I can't miss third period on Thursday. I have band practice on Monday, Tuesday and Thursday. Just pick any other day and I'll let you know if it works." You get the picture. After a few rounds of this craziness I had to tap out. I have enough trouble being my own personal assistant, I sure as heck didn't have time to take on additional clients!

It finally occurred to me that my daughter had a phone and she knew her schedule. I shared the relevant contact information with her, and she was on her own to do what any teenager is perfectly capable of doing. Of course, she hated it. After a lot of procrastination, she finally told me how uncomfortable she felt. She didn't know what to say or ask, and she worried about sounding stupid or making a mistake. So I sat down with her and we practiced the calls. I told her what they would likely say/ask and what she'd need to request. As you would expect, her apprehension and dread diminished with every successful call she made.

My younger daughter struggled with remembering important things she needed for school. Even if it was set out ahead of time and ready to go, it still might not make it out the door with her. I can't count how many times I had to drop what I was doing and bring things to her during middle school, but I know it was too many. When she entered high school, I told her I'd still help her, but I couldn't continue to bail her out every time she forgot something. Instead, I gave her two (and only two!) "saves" that she could use during the school year, and I recommended that she keep them in reserve for the big stuff. As a result, I no longer get called or texted (or both) to bring her a forgotten lunch, or jacket, or homework assignment.

We've both learned to be okay with her experiencing the natural consequences of her actions, or inaction. If she forgets her lunch, she may be hungrier than usual when she gets home, but she'll survive. If she forgets her jacket on a fall day, she'll be uncomfortable, but she won't freeze to death. If she forgets a homework assignment, she may have to do some extra credit work to make up for it but she won't fail the grade. Letting our kids deal with the consequences of their choices and behavior is what helps them become independent and responsible, and it really helps to improve their memory.

Of course, a forgotten lunch is one thing, but forgotten school assignments are entirely another. The instinct to help children with school is probably one of the most challenging for any parent to override with any consistency, especially when our children are struggling academically. We often feel the need to *helicopter*—hover over, keep track of when assignments are due, and remind them and remind them, again and again. It's stressful for parents and students alike. I was really stuck when it came to this dilemma. I felt an overwhelming concern about the consequences of missed assignments and poor test grades, so I constantly *encouraged* my kids to keep up with their work. They had another word for it: *nagging*.

Eventually I realized that my nagging was fueled by my own fear and concern, but it wasn't necessarily grounded in reality. I was laser-focused on the deadlines and negative consequences of missing them, but I didn't know what my kids were actually *doing* about their assignments.

They told me that they had everything under control, but based on past experience, and without more to go on, I just didn't believe them. Finally, we talked about it. I explained to them that the more they demonstrated they were being responsible, the more I would back off. They told me that the more I backed off, the more responsible they would be. We decided to meet in the middle: they would tell me more about *how* they were completing their assignments, and I would cut back on the help I provided them—aka nagging. With more talking and less hovering, our interactions about school became far less tense.

INDULGING

Children *need* certain things to live and thrive. Food and water, love and affection, and learning opportunities are all necessities. Children (and adults) *want* many other things. Smartphones, designer clothes, luxury cars, and expensive vacations are all niceties. Even though we sometimes hear people say they *will just die* without certain niceties, no one ever has. Parents should provide children with all the things they *need*, and should provide children with things they *want* up to a reasonable point. Unfortunately, no one can say for certain where that reasonable point is. It differs for every family based on their financial situation and unique set of values. What is reasonable for one family might be totally unreasonable for another family.

As a parent, I struggle with how much to indulge my children. I want them to be happy, I like giving them things they want, and I really hate saying "no" to them. But I am also keenly aware of the hidden costs that can come with overindulging children. In the same way that unearned, overused, or inappropriate praise (a form of overindulgence) can have a negative impact on students and their performance, overindulging children financially can have negative consequences, too.

One unintended consequence of overindulgence is that it interferes with the development of a child's critical life skills. Children who have everything given to them often do not understand or appreciate the amount of hard work that is required in life to achieve success. When they begin to struggle academically, they expect the solution to be handed to them and may not understand what they need to do to improve or be willing to do the work necessary.

If financial incentives are used to reward students for performance, it can make a child's motivation to learn entirely extrinsic. I've known of families who paid children for getting good grades, promised ski trips for straight As, and even offered an expensive sports car to their child if he graduated at the top of his class. While there is nothing inherently wrong with offering small incentives as a reward for hard work, overindulgent rewards for outcomes generally are ineffective and can do harm to a child's sense of self-reliance and self-esteem.

Another unintended consequence of overindulgence is that it may cause children to develop feelings of dependency on their parents that can last well into adulthood. Overindulged children may develop feelings of entitlement or become callous to others who aren't as privileged. Despite outward appearance, many of these same children often feel like frauds because they know that they have not earned the luxuries they have.

What to do

First, keep in mind the difference between *needs* and *wants*. Your child *needs* physical and psychological safety, but they *want* the latest and greatest technological device. They can't live without the former, and they won't die without the latter.

As a parent, you have a duty to say "no" to your child every now and then. Sometimes this comes in response to a direct request, other times it comes in the form of simply not giving them something extravagant or unneeded, which they may not even have asked for. Even if your family doesn't have to worry about how to afford such things, saying "no" to some things makes kids appreciate the things you say "yes" to all the more.

PRIORITIZING

While parents often think of overindulging children in financial terms, there are other ways that we overindulge them, such as giving them too much of our time and energy, especially when it comes to their *wants* rather than their *needs*.

As you've been instructed on every flight before takeoff: "In case of a loss in cabin pressure, put on your own oxygen mask before helping others." There's probably not a parent alive who hasn't experienced psychological and physical fatigue following an intense stretch of helping and prioritizing others (most often their own family members). If this is the norm for you, be aware that as your personal well-being declines, so does your ability to be helpful.

As parents, we do for our kids, but sometimes we do too much. It could be something as simple as your daughter sitting at the kitchen counter and asking you to get her a glass of water while you're busy fixing dinner. That may seem like no big deal, and you're usually happy to help her out, but realize that this reflects certain expectations your kids have of you.

Children often expect that you'll drop everything to do something for them which they are perfectly capable of doing themselves. They often expect that you'll change *your* schedule to accommodate *their* schedule. Sometimes these requests are reasonable and necessary, and you'll do what you can to be helpful. But other times there is really no justification to the idea that their needs are more valid or important than yours. Of course you want to be nice and helpful to your child, but if you feel you are being taken advantage of then you may be overindulging them and unreasonably prioritizing them ahead of yourself.

What to Do

You have to become a little "selfish." Understand that you only have a limited amount of time and energy to accomplish everything that needs to be done. When you prioritize your kids over everything else in your life, something loses out. It might be your job, your marriage, or your own mental health. Implementing reasonable limits to your limited personal resources does not deprive your children of anything they *need*, it just allocates resources to ensure that you maintain a healthy balance in your own life.

When I first became selfish (at least that's how it initially felt to me), I was self-conscious about my intentional decision to choose myself over my kids. Even now, years later, I am aware whenever I make that choice, and it still makes me a little uneasy. But what I've learned is that I am less resentful of, and more appreciated by, my children when I am a little selfish. The times I've said "no" to something that would interfere with my own schedule gave them insight into the fact that I have a life, and that they are not the center of the universe. Without any direct instruction, they now ask nicely when they want me to do something for them, instead of just assuming I'm available 24/7 to be their chauffeur, maid, and executive chef. And, to be honest, being asked in this manner makes it much more likely that I *want* to find a way to help them out.

Mick Jagger said that you can't always get what you want. It is a healthy experience for children to learn that we will always give them what they need, and if their wants don't always come first, they'll be okay.

POWER STRUGGLES

The power struggles parents have with adolescents may seem new because of their intensity, but they are really just an extension of the struggles you've had with them since their birth. Remember the old days when struggles revolved around taking a nap, or eating carrots, or picking up toys? These struggles were difficult for sure, but they were relatively low-impact and extremely manageable when compared to the type of issues that crop up with adolescents.

The stakes increase exponentially when we have to talk about driving, drugs, alcohol, tobacco, screen time, sex, grades, jobs, money, and peer groups. While we may be well-versed in parenting to get our kids to do what we want, the battle escalates to a fever pitch in the tween and teen years as their pre-frontal cortex becomes more developed and they are able to throw logical arguments at us, and not just temper tantrums. Since we are now dealing with half-child/half-adult creatures instead of small children, it makes sense to think a little about our approach to parenting and consider what has worked in the past and what will work best going forward.

PARENTING STYLES

It may seem that everyone's parenting style is unique, and to an extent they are, but research has uncovered four basic parenting styles: *authoritarian, authoritative, permissive,* and *neglectful.*

That last parenting style—*neglectful* parenting—involves a range of devastating behaviors, from not meeting the physical or emotional needs of a child to outright abusive behavior. I seriously doubt that anyone reading this book falls into the neglectful category, so I'm going to focus on the first three styles.

Authoritarian parenting is characterized by a "my way or the highway" approach to rules and expectations. This is, for the most part, a unidirectional communication style that expects children to do as they are told, show deference to and respect for authority figures, and generally fall into line with parental expectations. Think high structure/low warmth.

Permissive parenting is the "I want to be your friend" approach. Permissive parents tend to have relatively lax rules, if they have any at all. They tend to go easy on their kids' misbehaviors, see the misbehavior as funny or cute, or rationalize that "kids will be kids!" Think high warmth/low structure.

Authoritative parents are firm, but warm in their parenting approach. They maintain authority but do so in a manner that validates and includes their child in problem solving and decision making. For example, a misbehavior may be addressed through a discussion of why the child behaved the way they did, why the behavior was inappropriate or wrong, what a better choice would be and the appropriate consequence for the infraction. Think structure and warmth.

CONSISTENCY, STRUCTURE, AND UNCONDITIONAL LOVE

Research suggests that consistency, structure and unconditional love are critical to the development of a positive self-concept in our kids. For a child, knowing what is expected of them, and what they can expect from their parents, helps them make the connection between how they choose to behave and the types of consequences they can expect to receive. If you break a rule, expect an appropriate consequence. Every. Single. Time.

Kids may balk at the rules and consequences, but they need them. The consistency in expectations and consequences serves as a form of scaffolding that provides structure for them as they learn how to make decisions for themselves. It makes them feel safe and secure.

Unconditional love is usually the default type of love given from parent to child. However, there are cases of parents who dole out their love conditionally, based on the behavior of the child. Conditional love may be shown for good grades and accomplishments, but withheld when a child makes mistakes, falls short of expectations, or misbehaves. Compare that to a child who is loved unconditionally for who they are, not for what they do or don't do. It should come as no surprise that children who experience unconditional love from their parents will have higher self-esteem and confidence than those raised with love offered to them on a conditional basis.

LIFE SKILLS

Most disintegrating students lack basic skills that they need in order to succeed in school. Many appear to lack motivation as well, but this apparent lack of motivation is often the result of paralysis brought on by the student not understanding what is wrong or how to address the challenges they are facing. These are students who have reached their rigor tipping point and feel incapable of meeting the high expectations that have been set for them, by themselves and by others.

These students need help in two different areas: academic skills and life skills.

> Sam loved high school; he liked hanging out with his friends, he was an outstanding running back on the football team, and he even had his first real girlfriend. What wasn't going well for Sam were his classes. It's not that he didn't like his courses; he thought they were interesting, and he liked most of his teachers. But he was struggling

to keep up, to remember everything that had to be done (and when), and he was forgetting to complete and turn in assignments. Sam was also having trouble sleeping and his lack of sleep made it hard for him to pay attention in class.

Sam wanted to do well, but he always felt like he was running on a muddy field. He couldn't get his footing and felt like he wasn't making any progress toward the goal line. He didn't know how to deal with everything and was too proud and embarrassed to ask for help. Eventually it became so overwhelming that he just felt paralyzed and unable to do anything. This caused his anxiety to build up which interfered with his sleep even more.

Sam's mom was concerned about his grades, but she was much more concerned about his anxiety and lack of sleep. She tried to offer advice and bent over backwards to take as much burden off him as she could. She became a *snowplow parent*, removing as many obstacles from Sam's way as possible. She did his laundry, packed his lunches, and occasionally, when she felt especially brave, went into his bedroom and bathroom to give them a cleaning. She made his appointments, kept his calendar, and reminded him about everything he needed to do. But Sam's paralysis persisted, and he became sulky and sometimes he got angry for no specific reason. About halfway through the semester he was in danger of failing two of his AP classes and had low *B*s in all his other courses.

Sam's problem wasn't that he was lazy, or that he didn't care, or that he wasn't trying hard enough. What Sam lacked were skills— skills that he had never needed before and some he had never been told about, much less taught how to use. He didn't keep a calendar, didn't have a good system for recording and planning his assignments, didn't know how to prioritize tasks, and didn't have experience studying new and challenging material or a strategy for doing it.

Sam could learn those skills easily enough, with some proper coaching, but unfortunately, they wouldn't help him much in his current state of mind. Sam appreciated what his mom was trying to do for him, but at the same time her efforts to make life "easy" for him took away his sense of autonomy and self-control. He started to feel helpless and worthless. He felt like a disappointment to himself and his family. To the outside world, Sam looked lazy and unmotivated.

Sam's mom, with the best of intentions, was taking the wrong approach to helping Sam build up his self-esteem and confidence. She should have been giving him *more* opportunities to meet responsibilities at home, not less.* Though we can all understand why his mom was trying to shield him from additional work around the house, her overprotectiveness actually cultivated a whole new set of problems for Sam.

Children and young adults with little household responsibility or experience may have a difficult time transitioning to living outside their parents' home. Many college students know these people as their clueless, inconsiderate, messy roommate or, worse, they find themselves being that person. Setting up our kids to fail with roommates is not helpful and makes the transition to college, and to life, more difficult than it should be.

---

* I'm not a fan of the word *chore*. I sat my family down years ago and explained that our family and household operate as a unit, and we all have responsibilities to each other. So for us, *family responsibilities* replaced the word *chore*. I found my kids were much more likely to complete their *responsibilities* without too many reminders or too much complaining.

Doing everything for your child is not helping them, and more importantly it's not very fair to you either. You already work hard and piling all that extra work on top of what you're doing is going to wipe you out. Household tasks benefit everyone, so everyone should be pitching in as they are able.

RESPONSIBILITIES AND EXPECTATIONS

As a parent, you have to decide where to draw the line between not helping your child enough and helping them too much. For sure you don't want to just turn your kids loose on the world and let them live like feral cats, but most parents don't do that. In fact, in today's society most parents tend toward snowplowing. To avoid this tendency, give your children as much responsibility as they are capable of handling, while keeping the following suggestions in mind.

First, make sure the tasks you're giving your kids are age appropriate. If you entrust your four-year-old with the laundry, the best-case scenario is that no laundry will get done. (I don't even want to think about the worst-case scenario.)

Think in terms of what *your* child is *capable* of doing, and that will vary depending on their developmental age, maturity, and judgment. Here's a list of suggestions by age to get you started.

Elementary Age

- Helping with dinner (prep, setting and clearing table, loading dishwasher)

- Emptying small trash cans throughout the house

- Light monitor (checking that lights have been turned off)

- Putting toys and possessions away

- Dusting

- Bringing clothing to and from laundry room

- Wiping bathroom sink area

- Cleaning toilets

- Bagging grass or weeding

- Helping with pet maintenance (feeding, cleaning cages/tanks, brushing dogs)

Middle School Age

- Laundry

  o Step 1—Putting away their own laundry

o   Step 2—Sorting their own laundry

o   Step 3—Washing and drying their own laundry

- Emptying larger trash cans and taking bins to the curb (and bringing them back up)

- Vacuuming and mopping floors

- Emptying the dishwasher

- Washing cars

- Walking and bathing dogs

- Limited babysitting

High School Age

- Mowing the lawn

- Babysitting and childcare

- Maintaining cars (air pressure, oil changes, fueling)

- Running errands (personal and family)

- Scheduling their own appointments (haircut, tutoring, dentist)

- Painting or home improvement projects

- Moving furniture or other heavy lifting

- Small household repairs

This is not an exhaustive list, and of course I'm not suggesting that every child be required to do all of these things. It's just a guideline to the age-appropriateness of various household tasks. The younger our kids start (elementary school), the more they will want to help out and the easier it will be for them to accept bigger, more important responsibilities in adolescence and adulthood.

Second, don't announce the introduction of new responsibilities with a tirade about how you do everything, and nobody helps out. That will get you a short-term change at best. Instead, sit down for a family meeting and explain your position. Make sure they know that you're giving them responsibilities you know they're capable of doing, and that you'll help them learn how to do them well.

Your conversation may go something like this: "I need your help around the house. You're all capable kids and there are some jobs I know you can do. I'll explain what needs to be done and help you get started."

The idea is to avoid being bossy or punitive or

harsh, but to communicate your feelings and concerns in terms they can relate to. Present the situation not as your problem, but as a problem you're
all facing together. Invite your family to help prob-
lem-solve and come up with solutions that everyone
can live with, where everyone helps, and no one feels
overburdened.*

Might you get some pushback? Yes! Count on it.
But recognize that it's likely coming from a place of
fear. Your child's initial reaction may be that there's no
way they can learn—and then remember—to manage
these new responsibilities and to think that they're
just going to fail at something new. It will likely hit
many procrastination triggers: ambiguity, challenge
and frustration—and don't forget, it's not meaningful
to *them*. They may need to do it a few times to realize
it's not nearly as bad as they have imagined. Realizing
they *can* do it and they *are* helping, starts to build up
their self-confidence and decrease their resistance. As
they gain an incremental sense of control and autonomy over their life, their motivation will begin to

---

* Just a general note: Try not to lose it when your child messes
up … because they *will* mess up. They will break dishes, ruin
a favorite shirt, dent walls, and ding furniture. You've done it,
too. It's part of the learning process. Unless there was a reckless
disregard for safety and property involved, it's best to be
understanding and forgiving and move on. Otherwise, they may
start to avoid trying new or challenging things for fear that they
will mess up and get yelled at and feel terrible. No one likes to
feel incompetent and no one is perfect.

rebound, and they will be open to more challenges, at home and in school.

Laundry is a great example for learning competence. This is really a must-learn skill before being sent off to college, and there is no excuse for a college student to be bringing home laundry and expecting mom or dad to do it! Today most college laundry facilities are as nice and comfortable as hanging out in a Starbucks. We want our college students taking full advantage of this convenience and they can only do that if they've been taught how to do laundry.

Starting in middle school you can teach your child how to sort their clothes and bring them to the laundry room to be washed. Making a cheat sheet with some general guidelines and examples (including pictures) is helpful because otherwise they will ask you what to do. Every. Single. Time. But with the cheat sheet, you can remind them to refer to it to refresh their memory. This sends the message that they are in charge of understanding and learning this process and not to rely on you to do it for them.

With appropriate instruction and support it won't take long before your children can do many things as well as or maybe even better than you. But they have to be given the chance. And as you can imagine, a child who starts cleaning and helping with dishes in elementary school is going to be functioning at a much higher level and with more confidence when they are given even greater responsibilities in adolescence.

I advise parents to start giving age-appropriate responsibilities to kids as young as possible. Associate natural consequences with their compliance (or lack of compliance): "Forgot to wash your favorite jeans? Then wear the ones you hate." Keep the lines of communication open through family meetings where responsibilities are regularly discussed, evaluated and modified as warranted. The more your child feels central to the decision-making process the more invested they will be, and the more valued and capable they will feel.

RAISING RESPONSIBLE HUMANS

How we approach child-rearing has a significant impact on how well adjusted and successful our kids become when they enter adulthood. There are decades of research that support the finding that the best outcomes for our children are associated with being raised by authoritative parents who offer unconditional love. These positive outcomes range from good interpersonal relationships to academic and professional success. If we are trying to navigate the power struggles brought to the forefront during adolescence, authoritative parents are going to be in the best position to nurture and support their children.

Because adolescence and high school are game-changing experiences for both parents and kids, it's a great time for a parenting tune-up and reboot. It is helpful for parents to adjust or tweak their parenting approach as children shape-shift through their development. The first step is to acknowledge with your child that you understand that they are no longer a little kid who needs you to do everything for them. You know that they want and need to spread their wings, to try new things and to have more responsibility. They want you to trust them. This can be hard because trust is based on one's past behavior. So this must be explicitly communicated to them, too. They will need to earn your trust through their behavior.

Don't assume that they are making any such connections on their own. Once you've acknowledged your adolescent's needs and the importance of developing trust, then begin a conversation about expectations. Using all the information and suggestions provided thus far, come to an agreement on house rules and consequences. Putting these in writing and posting them in a central location is very helpful. It not only serves as a reminder, but also provides clarification and avoids disputes over who said or agreed to what during your initial conversation. While this agreement should be binding and executed with consistency, it should also be considered fluid, in that it will be revisited regularly and tweaked as things change (which they always do).

Establishing expectations, rules, and consequences that are applied with consistency and compassion will benefit you by decreasing the number and intensity of power struggles that occur between you and your adolescents. And it will benefit your kids by helping them to develop their self-control, take responsibility for their actions, learn from their mistakes, and feel a sense of self-confidence and self-efficacy that are crucial to becoming responsible humans.

CHAPTER 6

Building Trust

THE MIRACULOUS TRANSFORMATION

I HAVE ALWAYS BEEN fascinated by the changes we see in our children as they grow; physically and psychologically. In what seems like the blink of an eye they go from infancy to adolescence, and the miraculous transformation starts the moment they are born. We revel in their first smiles, coos, and finger grasps. They are truly remarkable! They continue to amaze us with their unfolding development; eventually holding up their heads, rolling over, crawling, walking, and talking. Language and mobility are definite game changers to parenting, and we figure out how to fill our toddlers' worlds with opportunities to learn and explore. With this new level of independence comes a new level of risk, and we establish boundaries and rules for safety and civility. "Don't touch the stove." "Say please when you ask for something." This type of responsive parenting tends to come to us naturally, stemming from eons of evolution-shaped strategies to keep our kin (and species) connected and alive. Early on we integrate these developmental milestones into our parenting routines without much upheaval.

And then along comes adolescence, and everything changes. The middle school and high school years are rough, on kids and parents. Not only do our children experience outward physical changes, they also experience significant changes in their brains, marking fundamental shifts in how they learn, think, and act.

The physical changes are obvious. As they enter into puberty it is typical to see a "thickening" in our kids. Children who used to be mostly skin and bones will start to gain weight and their clothes will get tight on them. Then they'll hit a growth spurt and the pudginess will turn into lean muscle. (And it's probably time to buy another pair of shoes, too.) As a mom, I remember noticing this most when waking my kids up in the morning. I would go in and think: "Who is this adult-size version of my child sleeping where my child should be?!"

The psychological changes our children experience during adolescence are equally dramatic. Prior to adolescence, your children likely considered you to be the center of their world. You were one of the smartest people they knew, and they looked to you for companionship, affection, support, advice, and instruction.

Unfortunately, when your child hits puberty you stop being the authority on everything, or their preferred source for information on anything. In fact, what you say often will be downright suspect. Instead of you, they begin to rely more heavily on their friends (and the internet) for information, advice, and opinions. What you think or feel does not mean nearly as much as it once did. As a parent, it can feel like your adolescent child thinks you to be the dumbest person on this or any other planet. If they are tempted to hear you out, they will surely check what you've said against what their friends at school think.

If these physical and psychological changes are big and significant to you, imagine how your child feels. It's likely you remember. And you remember feeling like only your friends could possibly understand what you were going through.

I sometimes think of adolescents as being like centaurs, the half-human/half-horse creature from Greek mythology, except adolescents are half-child/half-adult. Of course, I also think of them as being like Dr. Jekyll and Mr. Hyde. You'll know what I mean if you've ever had the experience of getting a warm hug one minute and then the next minute being told you're the worst parent ever.

When your centaur exhibits this Jekyll/Hyde behavior—and they all do it sooner or later—keep in mind that its perfectly normal and driven by their stage of brain development and puberty, not a desire to break your heart.

IT'S NOT ABOUT ME

For a number of years, I've kept a sticky note promi-
nently displayed on my bathroom mirror that says, IT'S
NOT ABOUT ME. It's a reminder to myself that whenever
I interact with my kids it helps to try, as best I can, to
see things from their vantage point, not mine. I try to
meet them where they are, not where I want them to be
or think they should be.

There is no way to take emotions out of parenting,
and sometimes we let our emotions get the best of us.
As parents, we all make mistakes. We all say and do
things that that we regret. Try as we might, it's not possible for any of us to be perfect.

It is possible, however, for us to learn new things
and to become better at parenting. The effort we put
in and the changes we make do not go unnoticed or
unappreciated by our kids. When we acknowledge to
our children that we find something to be hard or challenging, that we are willing to learn from our mistakes,
and that we are working to do our best, we are modeling a growth mindset. We are setting the stage for
them to go out and face challenges and to learn from
their own failures. This willingness to try and fail and
learn and grow is, I believe, one of the most important
aspects of successful parenting.

When dealing with adolescents it helps to see
things from their perspective, and neurodevelop-
mental research from the past decade has shed light

on how adolescents see things. One such finding is that teenagers tend to misinterpret facial expressions. Unlike adults, teens often interpret neutral, surprised, or fearful faces as being angry. Maybe you've had the experience of saying something to your teenager in a very matter-of-fact way and having them respond by yelling at you to stop being so mad. Once I understood this lovely little quirk of mental processing, instead of reacting defensively, I could channel the wisdom of my sticky note: "It's not about me. It's not about me. It's not about me."

I'm willing to bet you have a pretty good idea of what kind of mood your kids are in the minute they walk in the door and drop their backpacks. As parents, we've learned to read these nonverbal signals. What I've learned over time is how to use this knowledge to everyone's advantage. If I have something pressing I need to ask them about, I'll stop and take an emotional reading instead of hitting them with it the minute they walk in. If it's apparent my child feels emotionally raw or overwhelmed, I'll hold back what I want to talk about until they are in a better frame of mind. Don't be afraid to make that choice! It's not a matter of being controlled by your child's emotions, it's just a matter of understanding how their brains work.

THE 90-SECOND RULE

Whenever we have an intense emotional reaction to something, our body releases the stress hormone *cortisol*, which in turn triggers our fight or flight response. The chemical reaction caused by this normally lasts about 90 seconds, which gives our brain time to determine how best to react to what is happening. If someone jumps out and startles you, your body prepares itself to fight back or run away. If it turns out that it was just your child trying to be funny, then other parts of your brain will signal "all clear," the cortisol will dissipate, and you will calm down.

In practical terms, this means that when you and your child are having an intense emotional reaction to something, responding within the first 90 seconds is a bad idea. Doing so will likely trigger an escalation of emotions (theirs and yours), which will keep your stress response elevated. This results in an escalation of emotions, rather than a de-escalation. Not surprisingly, no one is well-served by this. Think of your brain as a snow globe that gets shaken as you become emotional. It takes about 90 seconds for the "snow" to settle and the storm to pass.

Since an adolescent's prefrontal cortex (thinking brain) is still maturing, they may find it especially difficult to control the intensity of their emotions. Any time you sense that an emotional escalation is occurring, take a breath and give yourself and the other person the extra 90 seconds needed to regain control of your emotions. This means not responding for at least a minute and a half when your child is yelling at you.

It's a good idea, before you do this, to explain to your kids what you'll be doing and why. In my case, I sat down with each of my adolescent children and explained how their current stage of brain development was influencing their emotions, their thinking, and their behavior. I told them that I would wait to reason with their thinking brain rather than argue with their emotional brain, and would not respond to them immediately while they were blowing up.

PERSONALITY

When I speak to groups of parents about improving communication with their adolescents, I always include a discussion on personality—the unique collection of traits that influence how each of us thinks, feels, and behaves. When we describe another person, we often use adjectives such as kind, helpful, outgoing, or funny. When enough adjectives clump together (using a statistical technique called a *factor analysis*), then we have confidence that these adjectives are representative of something bigger: a *personality trait*.

In psychology, there are a number of theories that address personality traits, with many psychologists believing that the *Big Five* theory of personality provides the best model available. The Big Five traits are: *Openness to Experience, Conscientiousness, Extroversion (positive emotions), Agreeableness* and *Neuroticism (negative emotions)*. These five personality traits can easily be recalled using the acronym *OCEAN*. It's important to note that all traits exist on a continuum. This helps to explain how only five dominant traits are able to account for the billions of individual variations in personality. The interesting thing about these five traits is that they appear to be universal. We find the Big Five across all cultures (even those without spoken language), as well as in several nonhuman animal species.

In my experience, the *extroversion* trait is the strongest driving force behind much of who we are and how we interact with others.

First theorized and popularized by the Swiss psychiatrist and psychoanalyst, Carl Jung, the extroversion trait is about an individual's preference for (and tolerance of) stimulation. Extroverts are born with a nervous system that tends to be chronically under-stimulated, and they seek stimulation from interaction with others. Introverts, who fall on the opposite extreme of the trait, tend to be chronically overstimulated, and find interaction with others draining rather than energizing. Extroverts energize themselves with people and activities. Introverts require solitude to replenish their energy. When left alone, extroverts tend to feel bored and antsy, while introverts feel rejuvenated.

To see how extroversion/introversion interacts in a family dynamic, let's look at the morning routine.

I'm an introvert, so I need to ease my way into the day through activities that manage my level of stimulation. If I don't, a loud alarm clock or a dog barking (or yelling at an always-running-late child) in the morning will be enough to derail my mood for the day. So my typical morning goes like this: I wake up before everyone else, make a cup of coffee, plan my day, cook and eat my scrambled eggs, and have another cup of coffee. Then I am ready to help my daughter get out the door for school. Then I shower and get on with my day.

But the extrovert in my house wakes up and needs to address their under-stimulation by talking to others, listening to music, and generally causing a commotion. I know this is going to happen, and that it's happening because they need that interaction to get moving. Which is why I get up early to have my quiet time first!

Levels of extroversion and introversion are often reflected in family dynamics. Have you ever been accused of having a "favorite" child? ("You like him more!") Though most of us vehemently deny it, if we think about where family members fall on the extroversion/introversion continuum, it's likely that the oft-referenced "favorite" is one who has a similar level of extroversion or introversion to us.*

Most people find it easier to see the perspective and understand the motives of someone who runs on the same operating system as themselves. If an introverted child is apprehensive about attending big social gatherings or joining a team, an introverted parent is less likely to misunderstand that behavior as anything other than managing their level of stimulation. An extroverted parent may not understand where their introverted child is coming from and interpret their behavior as being withdrawn or anti-social. If we regularly misunderstand each other on this fundamental level, it can feel like we just don't *get* the other person, which will affect closeness and communication.

The impact the extroversion/introversion trait can have is especially significant when neither of you can understand or explain your motivations. Extroverted kids may become easily bored when disconnected from others and forced to work in solitude and quiet. They may prefer background music or noise, or want someone to be near them while they work. They may thrive in a study group situation whether it's in-person or a virtual gathering. If we insist that our extroverted child come home and get started on

---

* When my kids ask, "Who's your favorite?" I respond it's whoever is not causing me grief in the moment.

homework by themselves, we may be setting them up to fail or, at the very least, not to do their best. To a parent unaware of the extroversion/introversion trait, the child may appear uncooperative or even lazy for not wanting to study after school. But the student who fights studying in silence, constantly seeks "distraction" with their friends on social media and becomes sullen or irritable when left alone may be expressing their need for more stimulation without even realizing why or how they are doing it.

The reverse, of course, is true for an introvert. Typically, after a long day of overstimulation in the classroom, lunchroom, the bus, and so on, an introverted child will need time to decompress and recharge so they can have the energy to do their homework or even engage in civil conversation with other family members. Insisting that an introverted child sit down and tell you all about their day as soon as they walk in the door is a losing proposition for both parent and child.

If you hadn't already, it's likely you are now thinking about how introversion and extroversion are showing up in your family. Family members who are described as "outgoing," who love to be around others, and who enjoy jumping into new activities are your extroverts. While those thought of as quiet, shy or slow to warm up, and "old soul" thinkers who enjoy their solitude are your introverts.

If we, as parents, are not in tune with the stimulation needs and energy levels of our kids we can misinterpret their behaviors as something we think is more within their control. We think that they just don't want to talk to us, that they don't care about their grades, that they hate to study, or that they're just being impolite. All of these assumptions might be wrong. Adjusting our schedules and expectations to take this key personality trait into account can make a world of difference.

IMPROVING COMMUNICATION

There are a number of proven techniques that can be used to improve communication and build trust. Improving communication within a family is an intentional and mindful process, and much of the heavy lifting will need to be done by you, the parent. But the payback will be worth it.

Here are some of the most important areas on which to focus:

- Undivided Attention

- Active Listening

- Empathy

- Acknowledging the Good

- Knowing Your Triggers

- Being Vulnerable

UNDIVIDED ATTENTION

Probably the most important thing we can do to improve communication with anyone is to give them our full, undivided attention. On more than one occasion I've been told that I agreed to something that I don't even remember discussing. Each and every time, it was because I was trying to have a conversation with someone while continuing to focus on something else: an email, getting a drawer unstuck, or simply being distracted by my own problems or concerns. These situations usually ended with me having to go back on my word, and my child being extremely upset and frustrated with me.

These days, giving undivided attention to someone or something may seem strange and unsettling. We are so used to multitasking that when we shift away from multiple things and focus on just one thing it feels somewhat alien. This is a skill we need to develop, practice, and get comfortable with.

Your undivided attention is a valuable commodity, and it's helpful to think of it as a gift that you're giving to someone. When you're in the middle of something and your kids come to speak to you, take a second to evaluate the level of need, importance, and significance, and respond accordingly. If your daughter is trying to explain the plot of the book she's reading or sharing a story about something someone did at school, you may know it's going to take a lot of your time and attention.

It's not a situation in which you need to drop every-thing, but it's important to her, so you want to really listen. If you're in the middle of doing something that you can wrap up, ask her to hold her thought just until you finish so you can give her your full attention. If it's going to have to wait, let her know when you will be available to listen, and be sure to follow through.

Your undivided attention gains superpower status when you add in active listening and empathy.

ACTIVE LISTENING

A technique used in counseling and conflict resolution, "active listening" requires the listener to fully concen-trate, understand, respond, and remember what has been said. For many people, the hardest part of active listening is keeping their mouth shut and really paying attention to everything the other person says.

When they have said what they want to say, restate what you've heard and how you understand it: "It sounds like you were disappointed in the way your friend handled that." Then wait to get the confirmation that *yes*, you understand it correctly, or *no*, you don't understand it correctly. If you don't understand it cor-rectly, let the other person explain it until you do.

When employing active listening, think of yourself as a detective gathering information and then clarify-ing the details and confirming the facts. Don't think about how to respond to the other person while they are talking, just listen and make sure you understand. Every reflection you offer should confirm what they've said; every clarification you request will signal to the other person that you are listening and making sure you understand.

EMPATHY

Empathy is the act of putting yourself in the shoes of another person and actually *feeling* what they feel, not just understanding it. Empathy is a much more powerful emotion than sympathy or compassion which involve feeling sorry for the situation of another without it taking on any personal significance. You can increase your empathetic powers by looking at situations from the other person's point of view and filtering the information you are gathering through their perspective. Consider their age, their personality and their history when trying to understand how they are feeling about, and interpreting, the situation.

This means factoring in your child's point of view when they describe an upsetting interaction they had with a friend. Consider everything from their age, their past experiences with this friend, their mood, and so on. Even though the problem may seem silly or small from your adult vantage point, when you take the time to consider the situation from their perspective you can better support your child.

Empathizing helps you formulate responses that the

other person will see as helpful. We can devise the best strategies to help someone when we see the problem as they see it.

ACKNOWLEDGING THE GOOD

Part of our role as parents is to teach good behavior to our children while correcting bad behavior. Thus, we become masters at telling our kids what they need to improve and pointing out what they are doing wrong. This is a necessary part of parenting, but no one likes to receive constant negative feedback, regardless of how well-intentioned that feedback might be.

We're all aware that our kids do admirable things, but we often don't take the extra step of letting them know it. At least, most of us don't do it often enough. It's important that, as parents, we remember to say (out loud) what we admire, appreciate, respect, and like about our child's behavior. It's important that we tell them what they are doing "right."

There's no upper limit here, as long as you're praising or acknowledging specific actions and behaviors instead of traits or talents. This is the "catch them doing something positive" parenting strategy, not the "tell them how awesome they are" strategy.

I inadvertently started a family tradition when my oldest was very young, around five years old, and his sister was almost three. We call it "Purple Plate." I wanted a way to reinforce in my children's minds the things that they liked about each other. (I suspected they would find their own ways to reinforce the things they didn't like.) So I bought a single purple dinner plate and we started taking turns using it each night at dinner. If you have the purple plate, then everyone else must say something that they appreciate or admire about you. Sound easy? You'd think—but imagine coming to the dinner table after you've gotten into it with someone. And now you have to come up with something positive to say about them . . . yeah, not so easy! BUT very impactful. My kids' question before every dinner was always "Who's Purple Plate tonight?" To this day, over a decade and a half later, we still do our Purple Plate ritual when we are together as a family for dinner.

Everyone likes to hear positive things about themselves, and we need to let our kids know that we see the good in them and that we appreciate their efforts.*

KNOWING YOUR TRIGGERS

If your child knows that college is very important to you, then they also know that the easiest way to get you to go off the deep end is to say, "I'm not sure I even

---

* My son recently graduated from college. Part of his graduation gift was one of our purple plates with letters from each family member sharing our appreciation and admiration for him.

want to go to college. My manager at Burger King says I can keep getting promoted, so I don't really see the point when all I need is a high school diploma." It's like putting a match to a fuse, and your child can just step back and wait for the explosion—*kaboom!*

Why would our children want us to explode when they have to know they will get singed, or worse, in the resulting fireball? Rest assured that if it wasn't rewarding to them in some way, they wouldn't do it. Think about it this way: if you were just encouraging (nagging) your child about writing their essays, or studying for the SATs, or talking to their counselor about the form they need to return, you may have *triggered* one of your child's current anxieties or concerns. There's no more effective way for your child to shut this topic down than to set you off with one of your own triggers, so they push a reliable button. Brilliant! It's unpleasant and unproductive, but very effective.

Our children observe us closely for their entire lives, and they figure out what makes us tick. It's in their best interest to do this. It's part of their job description as Child to watch the adults in their life to learn, model, and internalize what they see. This is a huge part of the developmental process, so they're not being sneaky or malicious in garnering this information on us, but they do sometimes use it in retaliation or to deflect our attention away from something else.

The best defense against being triggered is to acknowledge that certain things trigger you and to recognize what those things are. This requires an honest evaluation of past conflicts. You must first identify what tends to "set you off" and uncover the root emotions or fears underlying your strong reaction. Then it's a matter of figuring out what to do with this emotional baggage. I have found that vulnerability is the key to this reckoning

BEING VULNERABLE

Effective communication requires vulnerability—openness and honesty—from all parties involved.

To be more vulnerable in our parenting role requires that we be honest with ourselves and others about how we are reacting and feeling in a given situation. Just like our children's, our defenses are at the ready to come to the rescue whenever our self-image is threatened. Even the least athletic among us can engage in some impressive mental gymnastics to put a good spin on whatever is causing us to experience a perceived assault on our ego. Although being defensive and avoiding or ignoring what's bothering us sometimes makes us feel better, it doesn't help us solve any problems.

The fix is twofold. First, it's important to recognize the psychological discomfort or threat that we're feeling, and then make an honest evaluation of what's behind the feeling. This is the challenging part. Oftentimes it is necessary to acknowledge that we feel threatened, frightened, inadequate, or unworthy. These are not comfortable feelings to have about ourselves. But, if we take it a step further and ask why we feel this way and try to answer honestly, we begin to experience healthy vulnerability, which paves the way for better problem solving and communication.

Imagine the following situation. Holly (almost sixteen years old), asked her mom if she could attend a concert with some friends. Holly and her friends are responsible kids, all-around good eggs. They're desperate to see their favorite artist, who is playing at a huge outdoor arena over an hour away from their suburban homes. Holly's friend Rachel, a junior and seventeen, is planning to drive. The girls would leave in the late afternoon and likely return home close to midnight. "Pleeeeeease??"

While I haven't experienced this exact scenario, I have seen similar ones. My gut reaction is usually fear and big-time anxiety. When my gut signals my brain to turn on the red flashing lights and sound the alarm, my knee-jerk response to my child is "No!" As I'm sure you can imagine, this is rarely well received, and crying, yelling, and pleading consume our every waking hour for what feels like an eternity. The stress of the reaction inevitably raises the option of caving, which might be very attractive, especially if we suspect we might have said, "No!" simply out of fear.

This would be a perfect time to practice vulnerability. It's the time to come clean and be honest with your child regarding your response and reaction. If your response was driven by fear, share that information. Outlining your very specific concerns and fears is the first step to resolving the conflict.

I might say something like: "I am uncomfortable with you driving through Atlanta with a relatively inexperienced driver." After she counters with a passionate defense of her friend's stellar driving abilities I might fully confess: "I'm worried about people who might try to take advantage of three girls alone, I'm concerned about your safety at such a large venue so far away from home, I'm worried about violence breaking out, I'm worried, I'm worried, I'm worried!"

It is sometimes funny how two individuals can have completely opposite views of a situation. All Holly, or any other child, will be considering is how much fun and how exciting it will be to go see this amazing concert with her friends. Fear and excitement are two sides to the same coin, and it's what we tell ourselves that determines which side of the coin lands facing up.

If Holly's mom can refrain from an immediate response of "Yes" or "No," telling Holly that she needs some time to consider how she feels about it before she answers, she can take that time to do a gut check. What happens next will vary by parent, by child, and by situation. There are many factors that will influence the final decision: How responsible is your child? Has there been a lot of crime around the concert venue? How much are the tickets? What is scheduled for the next morning?

But the most important thing is to make sure, for yourself and your child, that your final decision comes from a place of honesty. If Holly's mom cannot tolerate the thought of her daughter being in what she sees as a potentially unsafe situation inappropriate to her age, then she needs to tell her so. If she hides her true feelings behind vague (authoritarian) rationalizations like "Because I said so" or "You're too young," the decision is more likely to be met with resistance, frustration, and anger.

That's not to say that when you are vulnerable and honest with your child everything will be hunky dory! There will likely be disappointment and frustration, but because you've laid out your feelings, it's less likely you'll see anger or resentment from your child. Using this approach also helps you protect yourself from becoming triggered because you can step back and consider the things that tend to set off your mental alarms.

Being vulnerable is easier for some than for others. Some parents—not to mention some kids—find it very uncomfortable and threatening to openly express their feelings in a face-to-face conversation. If this sounds like someone in your family, I have a suggestion: Write it down. Get a spiral notebook or blank journal that can be used to pass a conversation back and forth. For instance, mom or dad can write out their observations and concerns, and ask some open-ended questions, and end with an invitation for the child to respond back either in person or in writing. Then put the book someplace where only that child will see it. You might also try texting each other, even if you are sitting side by side on the same sofa.

Don't rush this. It may take a few days for your children to process what you've shared and to decide if, when, and how they want to respond. The nice thing about this technique is that it feels more low stakes than a face-to-face conversation. This can be a game changer for both parents and children who keep putting off what they perceive will be difficult and challenging conversations.

Being as open, honest, and vulnerable as possible when communicating with your adolescents will go a long way to improving the quality of your parent/child conversations and building trust. Once the quality of the communication improves, a more productive and meaningful connection can grow.

COOPERATIVE PROBLEM SOLVING

Parents are good problem solvers—sometimes too good. Solving problems has been high on the list of our parenting responsibilities since day one, because infants, toddlers, and younger kids often need us to step in and help them out.

But as our children get older and become more

capable, our instinct for problem solving can itself become a problem if we continue to treat our adolescent children like little kids. As our kids grow, they need the experience of doing what they can for themselves. By the time they are tweens and teens they can and should begin to solve many (if not most) of their own problems, and we need to step aside and let them do it. This doesn't mean that they are on their own with no help from mom or dad, but they should be in the driver's seat, with us along for the ride (to help in case they get totally lost or have a flat tire).

Think of your role shifting from *explainer* and *solver*, to *interviewer* and *facilitator*. Instead of telling your adolescent children what to do and how to do it, ask questions that will guide their thinking to a clear understanding of their problem and possible solutions.

The types of questions and prompts will shift as your children get older. Middle schoolers will need more problem-solving support as they experience novel social stressors in conjunction with their own physical and psychological changes. For this age group, parents may have to suggest solutions, but it's important to talk through why those solutions may be preferable to other options. This is a skill-building process that helps a tween begin to think more critically, weigh options, and evaluate consequences. By high school, they should be equipped to come up with good solutions on their own, with you playing a minimally supportive role.

CHAPTER 7

77 Tips to Be Productive and Well

ONE OF THE REASONS that I've been successful in helping students make the changes they need to be productive and well is that I don't just tell them *what* to do, I also explain *why* they should do it and *how* it will help them. When I explain to students *why* they are thinking or feeling the way they are, and *why* a strategy or skill will help them, I get their buy in. This makes them more interested in developing and implementing solutions, which results in a willingness to try new things, some of which they may find challenging or even scary.

This chapter includes 77 Tips to Be Productive and Well, which you and your disintegrating student can use to get back on track. The tips in this chapter are written as if I were explaining them to a student; however, I would never consider throwing all of the tips at a student at one time without any context or explanation. It's much more effective to offer specific strategies, discuss the brain science involved, and provide supporting information that's directly related to specific challenges the student is facing.

These tips are grouped in the seven areas of skill deficits and counterproductive behaviors that are common among disintegrating students:

1. Organization (Tips 1–5)

2. Time Management (Tips 6–19)

3. Study Skills and Habits (Tips 20–44)

4. Mindset (Tips 45–50)

5. Stress (Tips 51–57)

6. Sleep (Tips 58–67)

7. Screens (Tips 68–77)

The 77 Tips to Be Productive and Well do not represent an exhaustive list, but for anyone trying to make significant improvements in their academic performance and general wellness they do provide an excellent starting place. It's not necessary to do everything suggested in order to see results. Incorporating any of the tips into your child's life will benefit them, and you. For now, read over the 77 Tips to Be Productive and Well and pick two or three that address the most urgent challenges you and your student are facing. Because not all of the tips are applicable to all ages, you may want to modify and tweak some of them to fit your child's specific situation and needs.

By now you're probably wondering if you should pass this book along to your child and have them read this chapter. I get asked this frequently and here's my advice: If your child is in middle school, high school, or college and has been asking for help, then they would absolutely benefit from reading through the tips that target their concerns. If your child has been rejecting offers of help and insists, "I've got this!" they will be less receptive to the invitation. Timing is everything!

So what is a parent to do?! First, I want to urge you to check that your expectations are reasonable. I think this is one of the more challenging things to do because in our learned-from-experience, middle-aged brains we easily grasp the value and utility of making changes for our own benefit. It makes sense and it doesn't seem that hard. Parents often say to me things like "I don't understand why my child doesn't do [fill in the blank], it would make their life so much easier!" And "How hard is it to write this stuff down?!" But here's the rub—our kids do not have learned-from-experience, middle-aged brains; they have those emotional, pleasure-seeking adolescent brains. So before you run to your kid and tell them what they *need* to do, try to recall how you felt as a teen and how you might have reacted to your parents trying to help in this way. A further annoyance is that our older teens often actually know some of this stuff. But just as with their under-standing of the perils of drinking alcohol, their behav-ior doesn't always match what they know.

Another way to approach helping your student buy in to these tips is to use your superpower of modeling what you want to see. Live out loud. Pick a tip from sleep strategies, time management, or screens, and tackle it yourself. Talk about what you're learning and how it's going—the ups and downs. Share openly so that your family can see the results. If you have a com-petitive streak in your family, you may find that others want to join you to see if they can do it, too—maybe better than you! This works for children of all ages.

If you have younger children, it will be easier for you to incorporate these strategies into your parenting and family structure, and it will reap benefits later on. If children grow up with a system to manage screen use or help them remember their chores and homework, then they will more readily embrace expectations around responsible screen usage and transition into a more self-directed time-management system in adolescence.

If you are met with stubborn resistance consider taking a scaled-down, slow, and incremental approach to implementing changes intended to help them. You may want to suggest very small, subtle shifts in the way something is done. For example, if your child is always on their phone in the car, ask that they do not get on their phone for short car rides, say, of less than 20 minutes. (Remember when car rides used to be a great opportunity to get that one-on-one time with our kids?) Often our kids are surprised by how good it feels to be off their screens. This may motivate improvements to their self-regulation and make them more open to other compromises around their devices.

The key takeaway is that less can be more: in other words, that baby steps are a powerful catalyst for change. You help your child most by having reasonable expectations and supporting them as needed. Meet them where they are, not where you think they should be or want them to be. Trust that they will get there in their own time, and help them along the way.

TIPS 1–5: ORGANIZATION

1. *Declutter:* Get rid of things you don't need so you can find the things you do need. Backpacks can easily become pits of despair. Remove anything that you don't use often. The goal is to throw out old papers, garbage, receipts, candy wrappers, tissues, whatever. Clean out binders, folders, and books. Get rid of everything from school that you don't need. Pick a day of the week to declutter and do it on that same day every week. Sunday is a

good choice because it gives the start of the week a sense of order. The first time you do it will take the longest; maybe 15–20 minutes, depending on how messy your bag is. Subsequent declutters should take five minutes or less. Completely empty and launder your backpack at least once a semester or whenever your Snickers candy bar melts and smashes all over the interior.

2. ***Give everything a home:*** Provide everything you own with its own home—a place for it to live safely and securely when you're not using it—so you'll know where it is when you need it. Find real estate for each item that is convenient and highly visual. To get started, identify one thing that you own, which you misplace frequently. It may be your car keys, your phone, or your wallet. Once you establish a home for that item, you can move on to another. Some items are jet setters. They are constantly traveling from room to room and often get lost. Phones are notoriously mobile in this way. If you are constantly searching

for your phone, splurge and give it multiple homes—perhaps one in every room that you frequent in your house. Perhaps it needs a home in the kitchen, a vacation home in the bedroom, and a third home in the family room. The key is to put things in the same place every time, so you know where they are. Practicing this kind of behavior will generalize into more intentional thoughts about how your life and world are organized and support additional positive changes over time.

3. ***Clean a little at a time:*** If you have a messy bedroom, dorm, or apartment, someone is probably nagging you to clean it up, even if it's just a voice in the back of your own head. Unfortunately, trying to clean a large area will be difficult and unpleasant, trigger procrastination, and quite possibly result in failure. The key to success is to approach big cleanups in smaller chunks. Identify a small cleanup task within the larger mess, set a timer for ten minutes, and GO! How you divide the mess is up to you.

It may be that you decide you'll pick up all of your books from the floor and put them on the bookshelf. It may be that you take an empty trash bag and just fill it with trash lying around. Or, you may spend ten minutes dealing with clothes lying all over the place and deciding what gets put away and what needs to be laundered. Do whatever works best for you.* Set reasonable expectations and allow yourself to practice and get better over time. And don't forget to give yourself a small reward for each round of successfully completed cleaning.

4. ***Develop a school organization system (S.O.S.):*** Everyone benefits from having a system for storing and finding schoolwork when they need it. Personalize your S.O.S. based on your own preferences. If you want to use binders, think about the amount of material you'll need to put in them to figure out what size binders will work

---

* This approach works well with younger children and can be especially helpful for children with ADHD, who will benefit from a specific small task with a timer to help them focus and make it less boring.

and how many to buy. Color-coding can help you organize your materials. First, assign each subject a color. For example, make red your color for math and then put everything associated with math in a red folder or binder. In your planner or calendar, color-code math assignments and test dates red so that when you see red your brain will automatically think *math*. This reduces the chance that papers will end up in the wrong binders and makes storing and finding materials more efficient. Try out various options until you find the right combination that suits your needs. Finding and using the system that feels right and supports your work is the ultimate goal.

5. *Set goals:* Set goals to help you identify priorities, organize your schedule, and manage your time. Goals should always be SMART: Specific, Measurable, Achievable, Relevant,

and Timed.* Setting a goal like "read more" sounds nice but isn't SMART because it's not *specific*, can't be *measured*, and isn't *timed*. It is easily *achievable* since reading one more page counts as *more*, but that's probably not what you had in mind when you set the goal. It's not at all clear whether or not it's *relevant*, since it doesn't specify what you'd be reading. A goal to "read all the Harry Potter books by the end of the month" is better because it's *specific*, *measurable*, and *timed*, but it falls short because it may not be *achievable* and may not be *relevant*. A goal to "read five pages from my history textbook every day for two weeks" is SMART, because it's very *specific*, easily *measurable*, definitely *achievable*, clearly *relevant*, and *timed*.

---

* There are several variations of the wording that makes up this acronym, but all are similar in their meaning and contribution. For example, in some variations the word *realistic* is used instead of *relevant*.

TIPS 6–19:
TIME MANAGEMENT

6.   *Keep a master calendar:* This will enable you to see the big picture of what the future has in store for you. It's the place where you write down all your major responsibilities—your must-dos—including important due dates, practices, appointments, family and social obligations, your work schedule, and travel plans. The format of the master calendar is not as crucial as making sure that everything gets on it. Some people prefer a whiteboard. Others like a large desktop calendar. Still others prefer a flip calendar, or the monthly calendar contained within their agenda. A simple, no cost option is to print a blank monthly template found on the internet. Once you've established your master calendar then you can begin to practice planning through the use of weekly and daily calendars.

7.   *Keep a weekly calendar:* Make it standard practice to rough out your weekly schedule every Sunday. Refer

to your master calendar to see the must dos for the week ahead, and then build your weekly schedule. First, write in your hard-time commitments, such as your job or practices or appointments. Next, look at the schoolwork you need to do and consider when it's due and how much time you will need to complete it. The simple act of recording and tracking your responsibilities across several formats will help your brain to understand and visualize time better and keep you on track, motivate you, and reduce your stress level.

8. *Keep a daily calendar:* Use your daily calendar to drill down and specifically allocate your waking hours. Break each day into 30-minute increments starting after school. Don't forget to include travel, meals, chores, relaxation, and all the other things that take time. Thinking about and recording the specifics of your day is helpful for a variety of reasons. First, it gets you thinking about your time in a more concrete and realistic manner. Second, it helps to

tame procrastination because you have committed to a plan to follow. Third, it's a great reality check for how much time things actually take. Using multiple calendars may seem redundant, but it's part of the process of improving your relationship with time.

9. ***Plan your day:*** Every morning, before you do anything else, write down three things you want to accomplish by the end of the day. This will give your day focus. As you make decisions throughout the day, consider how your choices will impact the three things you want to accomplish. At the end of the day check off what you accomplished, reflect on how things went, and use that information to make better plans and choices for the next day.

10. ***Try a pocket schedule:*** Some students find that a simple, uncomplicated, easily accessible system known as a "pocket schedule" works well. All you need is a piece of paper with a line drawn vertically down the center dividing the page in half lengthwise.

Label the left column TODAY and the right column LATER. The night before or morning of, take your paper and, on the TODAY side, record the day's requirements and commitments. List the assignments you need to turn in, appointments or practice times, and any other reminders or errands that you need to remember. The LATER column is for all the stuff that comes up during the day that you need to remember to do later—maybe a new assignment or a change to an assignment was made in class or a permission slip that needs to get a parent's signature is due. To use the pocket schedule effectively, keep it very handy (like in your pocket) so that you can easily access it to check what you need to do today, and to jot down the stuff that comes up for later. Treat that piece of paper like gold because it's valuable—like an extra brain in your pocket. When you get home transfer all of the LATER items onto your master calendar. Check over the TODAY list. Did anything not get done? Is it an opportunity lost, or can it be moved to tomorrow's TODAY column? This is a great chance to reflect on the day's accomplishments.*

11. ***Do a reality check:*** This is an exercise that will be helpful to establish a deeper understanding and appreciation of time. In general, people tend to underestimate how long tasks will take to complete. This is partly due to a flaw in human thinking referred to as the *planning fallacy.* The best way to avoid this is to always assume that whatever you plan to do will take longer than you think it will. A good rule of thumb for people starting out is to double (yes, double!) the amount of time you think any homework assignment, term paper, or other project will take. To improve your ability to accurately

---

* It is very helpful to use all the time-management tools—the master calendar, the weekly and daily calendars, and the pocket schedule—in the beginning. You are forming new thinking habits around your time and schedule. Within a few weeks, you should begin to notice the benefits. Over time you can wean off some of the calendar planning steps. The master calendar will remain necessary, but you may be able to phase out the weekly and daily calendars. You may also find that you can more efficiently manage traditional paper or smartphone planners and calendars.

estimate how much time something
will take you, jot down the task or
assignment and estimate how much
time you *think* it will take. When
you are finished, make notes on how
long it actually took. Note your start
and stop times and compare. Were
you close or way off base? If the task
took much longer than expected, ask
yourself, *Why?* Was it harder than
you thought it would be? Were you
unprepared (missing materials or
information)? Were you interrupted
or distracted? This type of thinking
will help bring into focus aspects of
how you work and break down the
sometimes overlooked aspects of a
project that require time to complete.
Once you begin to improve your time
estimations you can phase out this
exercise.

12. ***Think about your future self:*** Your
future self is you, just in the future.
It's the person you will become
based on the decisions you make and
the actions you take in the present
moment. If you put something off
today, your future self is going to have

to do it, and will be very upset, and probably, disappointed with you. If you are skeptical that developing a relationship between your current and future self is game changing, try this experiment: The next time you decide to put something off that you should be doing now, write a quick note to your future self, describing what you are putting off and why. When you finally do get around to doing it, read the note. How does your future self feel about having to do the thing your present self didn't do? Do you wish you had done it when you first wrote the note? Were your reasons for putting it off justified? How much did the task weigh on your mind between the time you decided to put it off and the time you finally did it? Do you wish you had just done it rather than procrastinated? The more you think in these terms, the more control you will gain over your level of motivation in the moment, and the more you will be able to avoid procrastination.

13. ***Keep time and energy logs:*** A *time log* is simply a grid or spreadsheet divided

into 30-minute blocks over a 24-hour period. Your job is to jot down a brief description of how you spent the bulk of each 30-minute block. (It's not necessary to stop every half hour to write in the log; just go to the log a few times a day and fill in the past few hours.) An *energy log* supplements the time log as a way to record how energetic you feel during each time block, using a standardized rating scale. You can create your own scale or find one online. People tend to experience two peaks of energy each day, as well as two low periods. After a few days of recording your energy levels you will begin to see when your high-energy times are during the day, and when you are dragging. With this information, you can plan to do your most important work during high-energy times so that you can maximize your productivity and efficiency. Save your low-energy times for low-impact tasks and relaxation. After completing the logs for a minimum of three days, including at least one weekend day, look over your data. How are you spending the bulk of your waking time? Are you surprised at how much you are napping or playing video games or checking your phone? Are you getting enough sleep? The nitty-gritty details of how we spend our time tends to be somewhat elusive to us until we make the conscious effort to pay attention to what we do. Use this information to consider trying out small changes to your routine and behavior. Small tweaks here can make a huge impact on productivity and stress.

14. ***Work like a PRO:*** PRO stands for Productive Response Opportunities and the PRO strategy helps you to take advantage of opportunities when your time has been "hijacked" by someone or something else. These are situations where you find yourself waiting for someone else, as a passenger on a long car ride, sitting in a waiting room, standing in line, and so on. Most people's default reaction in these situations is to engage with their smartphones to pass the time, which is rarely productive. Instead, work like a PRO and use these time

sucks to tackle something (anything) on your to-do list. Accomplish this by regularly prioritizing your tasks and taking work with you when you know you're likely to have time on your hands. You can even start and maintain a PRO list so that you can quickly pick from tasks and gather what you need to make progress on something.

15. *Use timers:* Use timers to help you focus your attention on specific tasks for short periods of time. Need to organize your backpack? Set a timer for 5 minutes and try to beat it. Have a chore to do? Set a timer to finish what you're currently involved in and set out to do the chore when the timer goes off. Need to be ready to leave in 30 minutes? Set a timer for 20 minutes so you're not rushing around in the final minutes. Break up your homework into timed chunks with short (timed) breaks in between study sessions. The use of timers that support tracking and visualizing your time will help a great deal. When choosing any timekeepers, opt for

analog over digital. Visualize time as a circle. Each completion of the circle represents an aspect of time, whether it's a minute, an hour, or twelve hours. Seeing time represented on an analog clock supports a more concrete visualization of time. A flat display of digits on a screen does not convey time in the same meaningful way.

16. *See it, do it:* Creating visual reminders through lists helps with memory and focus. Put sticky notes in places you frequently look, such as on your laptop, your nightstand, or your backpack. Use dry-erase markers to write notes to yourself on mirrors and glass surfaces in your bedroom or bathroom. Hang or place a whiteboard in a highly visible area where you can write yourself reminders. And, finally, if there's a routine that you have trouble following, write it out and laminate it and post it where it will be most visible to you.

17. *Identify your procrastination triggers:* When you find yourself in a situation

where you're procrastinating and it's bugging you, determine what is triggering it. Typically, it's going to be one or more of the following attributes that is triggering procrastination:

- The task is frustrating.

- The task is boring.

- The task is challenging or difficult.

- The task is unstructured or ambiguous.

- The task lacks personal meaning (it isn't personally rewarding).

Keep a procrastination list and consider which trigger(s) are associated with each task you are putting off, and what actions you can take to minimize the triggers so you can act.

18. ***Don't try to be perfect:*** In a learning environment, it is almost always better to do something wrong than to do nothing at all. Perfectionists often set unrealistic standards for

their work, and sometimes opt to do nothing rather than do something they're not sure is right. This is especially true when the work is challenging, difficult or frustrating. If you are perfectionistic, try to cultivate a growth mindset and view your abilities and talents as something you develop over time by taking on new challenges, asking for help and guidance, and accepting that mistakes and failures aren't necessarily bad things. Most important, don't put off doing something just because you may not be able to do it right the first time. Adopt the motto: *Progress, not perfection*. This is easier said than done, but the trick is to give yourself permission to break the task down and temporarily lower your standards. For example, if you are dreading a paper you need to write, set a timer for 15 or 20 minutes and just write anything to get started—without critiquing, judging, or editing. Then re-engage your high standards as you polish your work.

19. ***Start something, anything:*** Your
brain has an interesting quirk—it
doesn't like unfinished business.
Your brain seeks closure, so if you
start something your brain wants
to finish it, even when you move
onto something else. *Incubation* is
a term that describes when your
brain continuously works on solving
problems below your conscious
awareness and then inserts the
solution into your consciousness as
an awesome "Aha!" moment. You can
exploit this brain characteristic simply
by starting something. Consider that
big term paper you need to write.
If you say to yourself that you need
to write the entire term paper, your
brain is going to balk because it's
such a big task. But if you say you're
going to open a new document and
type the cover page and save it, your
brain is going to say, "Okay, no big
deal, I'll allow it." Once you've started
the term paper, your brain is going
to keep working on it subconsciously,
even when you are thinking about
something else. You've started an
open loop in your brain called "Term

Paper," and your brain will be itching to close that loop by completing it.

TIPS 20–44:
STUDY HABITS AND SKILLS

20. ***Pick the right place to study:*** Study in a place that is comfortable—but not too comfortable! The worst place you can study is your bed. First, it's way too comfortable. Second, when you associate studying with being in bed, your brain makes an unconscious pairing of the two which may result in poor sleep. Studying is a stressor, so if you study in bed then every time you get into your bed your brain will sound an alarm that activates your body's stress response to be on high alert. Instead of your bed, study at a desk or table or find a comfortable chair to sit in. If you are an introvert, find a place that is quiet. If you are an extrovert, look for a place with a little more activity. Either way, find a place that is well lit and not too warm. Choosing your study environment involves a lot of personal preference

which means that you need to consider many factors to help you to determine the most ideal setting for you. Of course, there's going to be a difference depending on age, with older students having more flexibility to study outside of their home environment.

21. *Monotask:* Doing one thing well is better than doing many things poorly. Your brain tricks you into feeling very productive and proud when you multitask, but studies show that people who monotask outperform people who multitask. When you multitask you quickly shift your attention from one task to another; from an email to a conversation, from a thought in your head to following a recipe, from reading a textbook to checking *Instagram*. Every shift results in lost productivity and poorer quality outcomes. Monotasking won't give you the rush you get from multitasking, but you will achieve higher quality results in less time. Try a blocking method to help you monotask. Schedule blocks of time

or days for certain tasks—homework, emails, exercise. Consider those times as a hard commitment to the assigned task. Engage friends and family to ask them to respect your availability and to help you stay accountable.

22. ***Pay attention:*** The human brain can process only so much incoming information at once, and there is a direct correlation between what you are paying attention to and what you learn. Use your monotasking strategy to shine a spotlight of attention on the thing you want to learn and leave everything else in the shadows. Attention is a resource that depletes with use so remember to take frequent breaks to replenish it.

23. ***Be active, not passive:*** Manipulate the information you want to learn, rather than just reading it. This is called *active studying*. It does not take more time, but it does require more effort and more focused attention. Done properly, *active studying* will enable you to learn information and retain it much longer. Here are examples of how to be more active:

- Create flashcards, practice quizzes, and guided notes.

- Explain or teach concepts to someone else, or to yourself in the mirror, or even to your pet or a stuffed animal.

- Work in a study group, and quiz or teach each other.

- Outline or chart major concepts and then recreate it from memory.

24. ***Think in pictures:*** Associate pictures with information you need to remember. Humans have a tremendous memory for images relative to our memory for spoken or written words. Anytime you can associate an image with a word, group of words, or concept, you have a better chance of remembering it for longer. When I teach the memory unit in my psychology class, I demonstrate this by presenting my students with a list of around twenty words, followed by a recall test. They tend to remember only the first five to nine words. Then I show them twenty images. When

asked to recall the images later, they easily and reliably differentiate the original images from similar, but slightly different images. More significant, when given retests days, weeks, or even months later they still show very good memory for the images, but poor memory for the words. Try incorporating doodles and drawings in your notes to help crystalize a concept and increase your recall. And pay attention to the images included in reading material to create efficient shortcuts to retrieving the information.

25. ***Build a memory palace:*** One of my favorite memory tricks is to create a "memory palace." The palace is any spatial configuration that you know well and can easily visualize in your mind. Now place images of things you want to remember throughout your palace and practice walking along and seeing all of them. Your memory palace could be your childhood home, your current home, your school building, or even an outdoor space like a golf course, running trail, or

your walking route around campus. This is a very personalized process. The more relevant and meaningful to you, the better this strategy works. When you need to recall the information, you can take a quick walk through your mental memory palace and visualize all the things you put in it. Another variation of this is to use your own body parts as the palace. For example, if you wanted to memorize the first dozen presidents of the United States in order, you could place George Washington on your head, John Adams on your right shoulder, Thomas Jefferson on your left shoulder, and so on.

26. **Sing a song:** If you can put information that you want to learn to the tune of "Twinkle, Twinkle Little Star" or any other song, do it. Music uses a different part of the brain than spoken language, and the combination of music and spoken language yields stronger, richer, and more lasting memories. I'm always impressed with the nineteen-year-olds in my college classes who can sing the states in

alphabetical order from the song they
learned in second grade!

27. ***Be bored:*** Plan some time to do
nothing, absolutely nothing. With the
pervasiveness of smartphones and
instantaneous *everything*, boredom has
become unnecessary and difficult to
tolerate for many of us. But consider
times when you are not "connected"—
in the shower, walking the dog,
drifting off to sleep—and think
about the ideas and connections that
sometimes pop into your head during
those moments. This is *incubation*
at work. These are the times when
people typically experience their
"Aha!" moments: "Oh, that's the name
of the thing I was trying to remember
yesterday that was driving me crazy!
Oh, wow, that's how I should start
the introduction to my Lit paper!
Hey, I just thought of a great idea
how to raise money for my club at
school . . . I can't believe I didn't
think of it before!" If we never allow
our brains to wander, to be bored
and unfocused, then the incubation
process is prevented from reaching

our conscious awareness. The solution to this self-imposed blockage is to be intentional in permitting yourself to be bored.

28. *Mind the middle:* Our brains can encode only so much information at a time. In fact, studies show that our working memory can hold only about five to nine chunks of information at any one time, and which chunks we remember depends on the circumstances. In experiments, when students were quickly shown a list of twenty words, their working memory only managed to remember the first few. Our tendency to remember things that come at the beginning of a series is called the *primacy effect*. If there was a short delay between the time the words were presented and the recall test, the students also tended to remember the last few words presented to them—a phenomenon known as the *recency effect*. Either way, the students were least likely to remember the words in the middle. When you sit down and plow through information for hours, there's a

whole lot of "middle" in that study session. To cut down on the middles, and create more of those memorable beginnings and endings, the key is to break up your study sessions into intervals of 20 to 40 minutes each. There's even a well-known method called the Pomodoro Technique which uses a timer to break tasks into 25-minute intervals followed by a short break. This spacing strategy is easy to use and, of course, there are several iOS and Android apps for it, too.

29. **Space it out:** *Distributed practice* is when you break up your studying across several days or weeks to get the information into your long-term memory. Studying for shorter intervals over a longer period is highly effective in achieving durable learning, and it's definitely more effective than "cramming" all of your studying into several hours the night before a test. I find most students are skeptical about spacing out their learning. They worry they'll forget what they study (or practice) if it's

not right before the test. The best way to be convinced is to try it! Let your master calendar help you to work backward to reap the benefits of distributing your learning.

30. *Interleave:* This is a strategy commonly used by math teachers that mixes up and intersperses former concepts and problems with new concepts and problems. Interleaving can be used when studying other subjects by periodically switching between topics, and by going back and reviewing older topics to refresh your memory of them. This helps you to recognize linkages between older and newer information and ensures that previously learned information is not forgotten. This strategy is particularly helpful in math classes because individual unit tests are often limited to what has been studied most recently, but final exams include problems that require you to use rules and formulas learned throughout the semester or year. Interleaving ensures that students remember older

concepts and problems even as new ones are added.

31. ***Accept textbooks for what they are:***
First, accept the fact that most textbooks are boring. They just are. This fact, coupled with the likelihood that your interest in the material may be low, puts assigned readings high up on the procrastination list.* Second, accept the fact that it takes about four-times longer to read from a textbook than from a book you read for pleasure. This is because the material included in a textbook is challenging and unfamiliar, and it takes the brain longer to process and understand new information. Now that you've accepted this, use some of the tricks below to make reading textbooks a little less awful.

32. ***Read textbooks a little bit at a time:***
Never tell yourself that you have to read an entire chapter. The reason for

---

* If I had to guess the percentage of my college students who actually read the assigned chapters, I would say it's probably less than 30 percent.

this is that if you say you're going to read an entire chapter then your brain is going to resist. You're also likely to become frustrated and impatient with how long it will take (4 times longer than a book you read for pleasure). Instead pick a manageable chunk of the chapter to tackle for 20 to 40 minutes and set a timer. Or choose to read one or two sections at a time, somewhere between five to ten pages. Reading in smaller chunks supports good learning and memory because it consolidates the information in a manner that is more likely to be encoded and retained. You can repeat this method of reading for as many times as you like as long as there's a short break between each of the sessions.

33. ***Read textbooks backward:*** Read the chapter review or summary *before* you read the chapter. This will give you advance notice of what the chapter is about, where it's going, what it will cover, and what you should be watching for. It will help you identify the most important concepts so you

can pay more attention when you read about them.

34. ***Test yourself on the textbook before you read it:*** Before you read a chapter, if there is a quiz at the end of the chapter try to answer the questions. It's likely that you won't know, or at least won't be sure of, many of the answers—that's okay. Your brain will feel good about any of the questions it answers correctly, and it will become curious and driven to know more about the questions it gets wrong. It's the same principle as all of the "pre-tests" you took throughout your schooling that you might have thought were pointless. Those pre-tests not only helped teachers evaluate the starting point and subsequent acquisition of knowledge, they primed your brain to look for the answers to the questions and gain understanding throughout the unit.

35. ***Read textbook headings and subheadings:*** After reading the chapter summary and trying to answer any questions at the end of the chapter, go through and read all the headings

and subheadings. Familiarize yourself
with the structure and general outline
and contents of the chapter. It's kind
of like when you travel to a new
destination by car and the ride there
always feels longer than the ride back
home. This is because the trip there
is unfamiliar, but you know what to
expect on the ride home. If your brain
gets a sense of where it's going in the
chapter, it will make the chapter seem
shorter and more enjoyable.

36. *Look at the pictures in textbooks:* Make
    a point to look at and understand
    the graphs, figures and pictures
    included in the chapter. They are
    there for a reason. In fact, publishers
    pay extra to include these elements.
    As I said earlier, humans have better
    memories for images and pictures,
    so the publishers include them to
    help anchor the concepts to visuals.
    Unfortunately, students report that
    they rarely even notice, let alone think
    about these added visuals. When
    asked, students report that they don't
    consider them part of the assigned
    reading. However, teachers will often

include questions that relate to a graph or figure on a test. Even more important, the memory of the visual from the chapter may be enough to jog your memory about the specifics in a way that helps you to recall more information.

37. ***Pick a method for note taking:*** The first step in note taking is to decide which method to use. The most widely used methods are the *outline format*, the *Cornell Method*, *concept/mind mapping*, and *charting*. It's not as important which method you choose as it is finding a system that is comfortable to use and captures the content being taught.

- The *outline method* organizes the new information into levels of topics and subtopics with supporting information that you've written in your own words as you understand it.

- With the *Cornell Method*, the paper is divided into three sections by a line down the center (two columns) and a line across the bottom leaving space below it. The right column is for describing concepts and information and the left column is for jotting down key words, questions, or dates associated with the information on the right. The space at the bottom of the page is for a summary of the information. This method requires more manipulation of the information and can be folded in half and used for self-testing.

- The *concept/mind mapping technique* involves writing down a central concept, idea, or keyword and then drawing connections to information, ideas, and pictures that link everything together. Some students find this to be a useful method to study characters, plot, and other aspects of literary works.

- *Charting* is simply using a table format with rows and columns to record new concepts and their associated descriptions and relevant information. Charting is a good way to consolidate and review information for comparison purposes (e.g., characteristics, strengths, and weaknesses of competing theories) and summary purposes (e.g., the steps in the scientific method).

38. *Take notes:* Seriously, you have to take notes. Students who take notes save time, are less stressed, and make better grades. Period. End of story.

39. ***Take notes as you read your textbook:*** Turn your reading from passive to active. This requires a piece of paper for each section. On the front side of the paper write the date, chapter number, section title, and page numbers. As you read the section summarize it on the paper. On the back of the paper, draw a horizontal line across the middle, dividing it in half. On the top half write down two or three questions that you could imagine being asked on the

material. On the bottom half, write
the corresponding answers. When
folded over this serves as a flashcard
to test your recall, and if you miss a
question, refer back to your summary.
If you still don't understand or can't
remember, then—and only then—do
you need to refer back to the textbook.
This strategy is incredibly powerful
for a couple of reasons. First, it
requires the active manipulation of
the new information provided in the
textbook. This increases the likelihood
of it being encoded, understood,
and remembered. Second, it is much
easier, and more effective, to review
the summary and questions than to
go back and reread the chapter.

40. *Develop a shorthand:* Develop your
own shorthand system so you can
take notes more quickly and easily.
Commonly used parts of speech
such as conjunctions and articles can
be shortened or left out completely.
Longer words can be shortened
with abbreviations. Initially, make a
small key in the corner of your notes
to indicate what your shorthand

represents until it becomes habit. Research has repeatedly shown that students who take notes by hand learn and remember more of the information than students who take notes on a laptop. Those using laptops tend to record information verbatim without giving it much thought, which is a very passive process. Taking notes by hand is a much more active process, which requires students to identify and summarize the main points. And I think you already know that *active* is more effective than *passive*!

41. *Identify your notes:* Mark your notes so you can keep track of them. Include the course name, date, and any other relevant information such as unit or chapter on every page. This may not seem necessary or relevant when you first start taking notes, but later on, when you have stacks of notebooks full of notes, you will find it very helpful to have a system that keeps track of what's what and where to find it.

42. ***Don't obsess over PowerPoints:*** Don't write down every word that's included on PowerPoint slides. This turns note-taking into the more passive activity of copying. The most important thing you need to do is listen to what the teacher is saying about each slide. Listen for phrases like "This is important" or "You'll see this again and again" or "Pay special attention to this." These are common ways teachers let you know that something is important, and you'll need to demonstrate knowledge of it on a future test.

43. ***Manipulate your notes:*** Reading and rereading notes is very passive, so you should do things to manipulate the information in your notes in order to make the learning more active. Some students manually rewrite or type their notes and color code them. Some turn written notes into concept maps, charts, or flashcards. The key is to understand the information in your notes, how it connects to other information, and to go back and ask questions or read the textbook to

fill in any information that may be missing or unclear. Many students just repeatedly read over their notes. While this is a great way to build familiarity, it does not necessarily lead to understanding. In fact, it contributes to the *illusion of fluency*, or the sense that you know *all* the information well. It's called an illusion because what you know well is just the information in your notes. You don't know what you don't know, and what you don't know might be a lot!

44. ***File your notes:*** File your notes after you've been tested on the material. Use an accordion folder to store notes by subject for the entire course. Once a unit is completed, clip your notes together in dated order and place them into the accordion folder. Include associated reference materials and supporting homework and assignments. This serves a couple of purposes. One, you can easily access completed work if you need to contest a recorded grade, and two, you can easily access your materials and avoid

the trap of rereading chapters when it's time to review for the final exam.

TIPS 45–50:
MINDSET

45. *Cultivate a growth mindset:* Having a *growth mindset* means that you are willing to exert effort, take on challenges, make mistakes, and ask for help. People who are willing to try—and willing to fail—become better thinkers, learners, and problem solvers. For most students this is the single most important change that can help them reach their academic potential. The key to shifting your mindset is to first understand how you are thinking about learning and your ability. If you are worried that you are no longer smart, concerned that what's worked in the past isn't working now, and you're comparing yourself to others who you think are judging you, then you likely have a fixed mindset and it's stressing you out. The good news is that you just need to replace some of those

thoughts with more helpful ones. For instance, if you tell yourself you're lazy because you're procrastinating on a big project, maybe, if you're honest, you aren't really sure what to do or how to do it and you're afraid to ask for help because you think you should be able to figure it out. You're not *lazy*; you're scared of being judged for struggling.

46. ***Focus on what you control and let go of everything else:*** You can control what you do, but you cannot control what other people do. Make changes in your own attitudes and behaviors, and don't try to change other people. Focusing on the actions, attitudes and behaviors of others will only frustrate you because you have little or no power to impact them. That's not to say that others don't have behaviors and attitudes that should be changed, but you benefit when you approach them from how you can respond to them rather than how you can change them. This is a tough tip to put into practice and takes a lot of effort and monitoring to alter your thinking

to minimize your focus on others' behaviors. But be patient with yourself and keep at it. You'll see the benefits before you know it. Get started by making a two-column list outlining the things within your control in one column and those things outside your control in the other.

47. *Be grateful:* Research shows that those who consistently practice intentional gratitude are on average, happier. And who couldn't use a little extra happiness? Start and end each day with a grateful thought. Whether you write it in a journal or do it in your head, practicing gratitude will make your internal dialogue more positive and could help you shift from a fixed to a growth mindset. There isn't a right or wrong way to be grateful as long as you're being intentional about it. Make gratitude family-friendly by keeping a jar in a central location and leaving notes of appreciation for each other to be read over a shared meal or activity. Or share what you're grateful for as you head off to bed each evening.

48. ***Be mindful:*** *Mindfulness* has become a bit of a buzzword recently, often associated with yogis and self-help books, and it's easy to dismiss it as another passing trend. However, if you look past the yoga mats and kale smoothies, you'll find that the idea itself has a lot of value to it. Being mindful means that you are paying attention to your present moment without distraction. It helps you focus on what is important. And it can lead to a happier life. After all, if you are not actively working on schoolwork at the moment, there is no need to let it stress you out. Practice mindfulness by taking short intentional breaks, where you engage all your senses and notice the sights, sounds, and sensations you are experiencing. This opens up your awareness and your thinking so that you can appreciate the "big picture" and be more grounded in the present moment.

49. ***Meditate:*** Being mindful can be thought of as a form of meditation, which can be done to improve attention and focus. Meditation

requires you to sit quietly and begin to pay attention to your breath—you inhale, pause, then exhale, pause and repeat. It's not rocket science, but most people are pretty bad at it, at first. If you start to meditate and then you lose track of your breathing and get derailed by a random thought then you're not doing it incorrectly, you just need more practice. The whole point of meditation is to develop our attention "muscle." With practice, you get better and better. Do it again and again and again. Making improvements to your thinking style requires some degree of mindfulness and/or meditation to be successful and long lasting.

50. *Cut yourself some slack:* No one is perfect, so we might as well embrace it. Forgive yourself generously and often. The more forgiving you can be of yourself, the more forgiving you can be of others. There's great power in embracing your humanness, including the good, the bad, and the ugly. When you mess up (and you *will* mess up), own it, forgive yourself for

it, learn from it, and move on. Easier said than done, I know. If you tend to have overly negative thoughts about yourself, if you're hypercritical, or have unrealistically high standards, here's a great exercise to try. First, take a moment to write down what you consider to be your personality or character strengths. If you really can't come up with any, ask your friends and family; they will know! Once you have your strengths in mind, before going to bed each night, write down one positive thing you did that day and which character strength(s) you used in the situation. Over time, you will come to appreciate your strengths and learn to cultivate and harness them to face challenges. Just as with gratitude, this is powerful when shared. Notice and praise the strengths you see in others and you're more likely to recognize them in yourself.

TIPS 51–57:
STRESS

51. ***Use stress to your advantage:***
Understanding how your stress
response can work for you or against
you based on how you think about
and approach the stressor can be
game changing. You have a choice that
begins in your own head, with what
you tell yourself about the stressor.
Instead of being scared that you're
going to fail a test, be excited to take it
and grateful that your body is giving
you the energy you need to perform at
your best. Not only is this response to
stress healthier, but it will make you
feel more in control, less likely to burn
out, and more resilient.

52. ***Get excited about fear:*** There's a fine
line between excitement and fear, and
that line is drawn by your thought
processes. People standing in line
for a roller coaster often feel both
excitement and fear at the same time.
People who feel only fear either don't
get in line at all or have to be dragged
onto the ride kicking and screaming.

People who feel excitement can't wait to get to the front of the line and will gladly ride the roller coaster over and over again. The fascinating thing is that the people feeling excitement and the people feeling fear will all be experiencing similar physical effects like a rapid heart rate, sweating, and butterflies in their stomachs. Just reframing your thoughts to appreciate that your stress is showing up to help you meet a challenge will flip your physiological response to be more supportive and healthier.

53. ***Don't star in dramas:*** You may not be able to avoid all the dramas that occur in middle and high school but try your best not to star in any of them. While drama, gossip, and intrigue make things interesting they also make things stressful, and stress will hijack your emotional brain, deplete your energy, and potentially impact your sleep. No one wants to risk losing friends, so this can be a tough one to navigate. Make a concerted effort to stay true to yourself and your values, don't betray confidences, and set clear

boundaries around your friendships.
Everyone makes mistakes (including
you), so be as quick to forgive as you
are to anger. And when you are angry,
hold off on responding or speaking
out until you can do it from a place of
calm and reason.

54. ***Reach out, connect, and help others:***
    Paradoxically, the busier and more
    stressed you are, the more you
    will benefit from reaching out to,
    connecting with, and helping others.
    If you are an animal lover, then
    volunteering at an animal shelter or
    a pet adoption event may be ideal.
    If you like children, then helping at
    day camps or tutoring would likely
    be a good fit. If kids and animals
    aren't your thing, volunteer at a
    local library or help out a teacher
    you admire in your school. Studies
    show that students who are under
    time pressures benefit from this type
    of work. It taps into the resources
    from your pro-social stress response,
    protects against burn out, and fosters
    resilience. If you're skeptical that
    adding more things to your schedule

will help, I encourage you to make a list of your interests outside of school and fit in what you can. If you can't fit anything in, then consider looking at your commitments and strive to find a balance between school and other interests and activities. You know what they say about all work and no play!

55. ***Have an escape plan to avoid peer pressure:*** If you are stressed about peer pressure, prepare an escape plan in advance and have it ready to use when you need it. Think about what you might be asked or encouraged to do and have some well-rehearsed responses at the ready. For some, humor works well to communicate that they're not interested in doing something. For others, feigning ignorance will do the trick. Still others might find righteous indignation to be effective. If you cannot think of any good comebacks to get you out of doing something, just "get sick." Fake nausea, a headache, or any other malady you can think of to get away

from the situation that's putting the pressure on you.

56. ***Use your parents to help you avoid peer pressure:*** If you are stressed about peer pressure and cannot think of any way to get yourself out of doing something you'd rather not do, let your parents help you. This requires you and your parents to develop a parent escape plan, perhaps a code word or phrase that could be texted to a parent if you want or need to get out of a situation. Your parents should agree in advance that they will not punish you for being in the undesirable situation, and they will be expected to assume the role of "bad cop," dragging you away against your will. This allows you to get out of the situation while saving face.

57. ***Learn to deal with test anxiety:*** Try some or all of the following strategies, techniques and mental hacks to reduce test anxiety:

- Remind yourself that the test is not going to kill you.

- Think of the test as a challenge and the stress you are feeling as helpful, giving you the energy and focus you need to do well.

- A few minutes before the test write down anything and everything that's running through your mind in the moment. Something about this task, known as a *brain dump*, appears to release the grip your emotional brain has over your thinking brain and allows you to regain focus and control.

- Chew peppermint gum or eat peppermint candy to help you focus during testing.

- Use a fidget spinner or other item to help with focus.

- Take intentional deep, slow breaths to help your brain relax.

- Avoid "drama" talk before the test. If any students are freaking out and talking about how they aren't prepared and are going to fail, ignore them.

- Watch a funny video right before the test. Laughing, even smiling, alters the chemicals in your brain for the better.

TIPS 58–67:
SLEEP

58. *Get more sleep:* Sleep more to improve your grades and increase your physical well-being. However much sleep you are getting, you probably aren't getting enough. Ideally you should be getting eight or nine hours of sleep each night, but strive for at least six. Chronic sleep deprivation will negatively impact all aspects of your physical and mental well-being. During sleep, the new information you were exposed to throughout the day becomes integrated and consolidated with previous learning. Lack of sleep negatively impacts all areas of your life, including mood, health, and thinking. Teenagers

already lack fully developed systems for self-regulation, and piling sleep deprivation on top of that results in impaired judgment, lack of self-control, poor decision making, and a weakened immune system. Consider sleep a critical part of studying. Without sleep, information fades away and cognitive functioning is impaired. You are better off studying for a few hours and getting a good night's sleep than staying up all night studying.

59. *Remake your bed:* Use your bed for its intended purpose: *sleeping.* Do not study or do homework in bed. Don't engage with social media or play video games in bed. Your brain is quick to associate the stress, anxiety, frustration, and excitement of these activities with being in bed. This means when you get into bed with the intention of sleeping your brain activates its unconscious association with other activities and interferes with your sleep.

60. *Adopt a bedtime routine:* Adopt a bedtime routine that signals your brain that sleep is coming. Drink a

warm, noncaffeinated beverage, read a couple of pages of a book (nothing too engaging or stressful), write in a journal, or complete a ritual to prepare yourself for the morning, such as laying out your clothes or writing reminders in your daily calendar for the next day. Whatever works for you and can be done every evening with regularity will become the routine that signals your brain to start getting ready for sleep.

61. *Turn out the lights:* Your caveman brain understands dark: "Dark mean sleep. Sleep good." Light can prevent or disrupt your sleep, even if it's only the faint glow from an alarm clock or other electronic devices. Use dim lighting as you prepare for bed, and turn out all the lights when you get in bed. If you have a television in your room, take it out. Not only will a TV encourage you to stay up later, if you fall asleep with it on, the light from the screen will interfere with your sleep quality. Eliminate all screen exposure at least 30 to 60 minutes before going to bed. The blue light emitted from

electronics mimics the light from the sun and tricks your brain into thinking it's daylight, which postpones the release of melatonin. Using the NIGHT MODE setting on devices helps a little, but it is still best to turn them off completely.

62. ***Keep a sleep log:*** To get an accurate picture of your sleep, keep a *sleep log* for a week. Track your caffeine intake, your bedtime, how long it takes you to fall asleep, how many times you wake during the night, what time you wake up in the morning, how refreshed you feel when you wake up, how many naps you take during the day, and how long they last. This will let you see patterns that may be contributing to sleep issues. Visit the National Sleep Foundation at www.sleepfoundation.org for a printable sleep log.

63. ***Don't hit the snooze button:*** As tempting as it may be, hitting the snooze button only makes your inevitable wake up more painful. It takes 90 to 100 minutes for a full cycle of sleep to complete. We feel refreshed when we wake from the early lighter

stages at the beginning of a sleep cycle, but feel groggy when we wake from the deeper, slow-wave stages that follow. Falling back asleep after hitting the snooze button increases the risk of awakening from a deeper sleep phase and experiencing *sleep inertia*, that groggy feeling that you just can't fully wake up. The resulting brain fog can stick around for several hours and negatively impact your productivity. You can decrease the likelihood of experiencing sleep inertia by getting the recommended amount of sleep and avoiding naps longer than 30 minutes. If you do find yourself waking up in a stupor, try to expose yourself to at least 10 minutes of bright light (preferably natural sunlight), consume some caffeine, listen to music, or step outside for a jolt of cold air.

64. *Keep it consistent:* The most effective way to reset your *circadian rhythm* (nature's sleep/wake cycle) is to keep a consistent bedtime and wake-up time. Every. Single. Day. Keeping these times consistent will help you fall

asleep and wake up more easily. If you can keep only one of these consistent, choose the wake-up time. This means not sleeping in late on the weekends to "catch up." Doing so only throws your circadian rhythm further out of step.

65. *Get some morning light:* If you find it hard to wake up in the morning, get a dose of natural light to nudge your wake cycle along. If no morning sun is available due to the season or time of day, consider purchasing a light therapy box. Getting some natural light can provide a mid-afternoon boost to your mood and energy as well. If you find yourself dragging during the day, go outside for a few minutes to boost your energy.

66. *Take a "nap-a-chino":* Naps that last from 10 to 40 minutes can reboot energy levels. If you find yourself dragging after lunch, take a short nap. The key is to keep the nap short. Longer naps will take you into the deeper stages of sleep that are hard to wake up from. A little caffeine before a short nap can help too. Caffeine takes 25 to 45 minutes to metabolize

in your system, so if you have a small
dose (some dark chocolate, a few
ounces of coffee or soda) before taking
a short nap, you'll wake up feeling
even more energized and alert.

67. ***Keep pencil and paper by your bed:***
Jot down any "Aha!" thoughts that
come to you as you're falling asleep or
waking up. And if you find yourself
worrying about something you can't
shake as you're trying to fall asleep,
dump it into the notebook and try
to forget about it for the time being.
Reassure your brain that it will be
there waiting for you in the morning.

TIPS 68–77:
SCREENS

68. ***Remove screens from your bedroom:***
Remove screens—smartphones,
tablets, computers, and televisions—
from your bedroom at least 30 to
60 minutes before you go to bed. If
you can't physically remove them,
turn them off. The light emitted

from screens interferes with our brain's release of the sleep hormone melatonin. Screen-free bedrooms help strengthen the association in your brain that bedrooms are for sleeping, not working, entertainment, or socializing. (Buy an analog alarm clock to replace the alarm on your phone if necessary.)

69. *Establish screen-free zones:* Establish zones where screens can't be used. These zones can be rooms in your house or times of day. For example, the bedroom can be designated a screen-free zone. So can the dinner table. You can also make 8–10 p.m. a screen-free zone. Establishing these zones for yourself and others strengthens your self-control and helps you to overcome the strong pull of your screens.

70. *Get back to nature:* Go outside and leave your screens inside. Nature has a strong connection to the most primitive and oldest parts of the human brain. Taking a hike, walking the dog, riding your bike, gardening, or reading outdoors can have a

powerful positive impact on your mental health.

71. *Socialize in person:* Make an effort to connect with people in person as much or more than you connect with them in the virtual world. Join a team, a club, or just hang out with your friends. Young people who have more face-to-face interactions with their peers and family members report better well-being and fewer negative emotions.

72. *Earn it:* Think of screen time as a reward instead of a right, and reward yourself with screen time only when you've earned it. When you finish a project, only then watch your favorite Netflix show. After you study for 90 minutes for your math exam, then spend 30 minutes on YouTube or Snapchat. But don't be too stingy, you can even reward yourself with brief phone checks during the five minute breaks you take between study intervals.

73. *Make your screens less exciting:* You can mute the appeal of your screens

by setting them to GRAYSCALE. Smartphone apps and video games are designed to elicit intermittent doses of dopamine, the pleasure chemical, to the degree that our brains can become dependent on and crave the next dose. Making screens a bit less exciting helps our brain resist their allure.

74. *Tame your notifications:* Go into your smartphone's settings and get rid of all the notifications that you don't need. Be very particular and intentional about what you *need* to be notified about, and decrease the intensity of all notifications by turning off sounds and badges and banners. Designate a time (or times) each day when you will check your phone to catch up. Enable DO NOT DISTURB or AIRPLANE MODE when you are studying. To minimize distractions while working on a computer, consider an internet blocker program like Freedom or try going offline when writing a paper to avoid the urge to check social media, play a quick video game, or watch a YouTube video (or ten of them).

75. ***Time it:*** Games and social media are designed to have no natural stopping points. Other things in life don't work like that. When you finish a chapter in a book, you know it. When you complete a worksheet, you know it. You never finish YouTube, or Snapchat, or Instagram, or Fortnite; there's always something else to see or do. This isn't accidental. The people who designed them don't want you to stop using them, ever. With no natural stopping points built into our screen world, we have to create them for ourselves. Use a timer to create a stopping point. When the timer goes off, you're done for now. Period.

76. ***Know your numbers:*** Smartphones now include features that track and report your usage. They enable you to understand how, and how much, you use your phone. How many times do you pick up your phone each day? How many hours do you spend on email, on social media, on communication apps, and on news sites? Get to know your numbers,

set SMART goals, and track your progress.

77. ***Connect with intent:*** This is the closest thing to a "digital detox" that I'll suggest. The idea is that you remove everything from your smartphone except what is absolutely necessary for you to function as a student or employee, and to maintain essential personal connections. For example, you may need to keep your school's portal app, your email, and text messaging. If so, then get rid of all the other apps that clutter up your phone and steal time from your life. Use just the bare bones version of your phone for a few weeks to see what you truly miss and need to add back. You may not miss the apps you thought you would, and you might enjoy the extra time you now have available to do other things. Intentionally customizing your phone to work *for* you rather than *against* you will help you control your screen time and your life.

MAKING CHANGES PERMANENT

Making significant changes in your adolescent's behavior can seem overwhelming. At least initially, you may need some help implementing changes and making them stick. This is where seeking outside help can be invaluable.

If your student is having trouble with an academic subject like algebra, consider a math tutor. If tutoring is unaffordable, see if their school offers tutoring from upper classmen or consider group tutoring sessions so you can split the cost.

If stress, anxiety, and/or depression are negatively impacting your child's academic and personal life, consider talking with a counselor or therapist. More and more parents are seeing the benefits of counseling for their adolescents. Personally, I think *all* teens benefit from having a trained, impartial, and objective adult to work with in order to gain a better understanding of themselves, their unique situation, and the people around them. As adolescents struggle to become adults they have a lot to figure out. Today more than ever, counseling and coaching can be instrumental in laying out a pathway to success and well-being.*

---

* Note that many well-intentioned parents try to help with issues affecting their children, but they often are too close to the situation and may even be part of the problem the student is experiencing. For this reason, parents often are not the ideal source of help.

The 77 Tips to Be Productive and Well provide the most effective and commonly used tools in my coaching tool box. If you have other strategies that have worked I'd love to hear about them! Share them with me at hello@drjannot.com.

A Final Note to Parents

WHEN I SPEAK TO GROUPS of parents, I always begin by expressing my concern that what I'm going to tell them may trigger feelings of anxiety, regret, and even guilt as they think about their own parenting styles and experiences. I know this because I often feel the same way when I attend parent lectures. As parents, we all tend to be very hard on ourselves, and worry a lot about what we might be doing wrong. For this reason, I'll repeat what I said earlier: *You are a rock star parent! You are trying. You are showing up. Every. Single. Day. And that's what matters most.*

My intention in writing this book was to explain some of the forces affecting our students, from developmental to cultural influences. I truly believe that when parents and students have the right information and tools to support growth, the outcome will always be positive. I've seen it time and time again. With a little guidance and help, struggling students get back on their feet and back on track stronger than ever.

Practicing the skills outlined in this book, in the

areas of communication particularly, will help you maintain a positive attitude and be more tolerant of normal adolescent behaviors. Recognizing when your child needs help and getting them that help is key. Whether it's coaching for study skills, counseling for anxiety, or treatment for depression. You are their advocate. Listen to their needs. Shake off any remnants you may have of a fixed mindset and be okay with asking for help. Model what you want your kids to see and learn. Be open and honest with them and be vulnerable. Let them learn from your successes and your failures. It is your most powerful tool.

Above all else, be patient. Be patient with yourself. Be patient with your child. Even the simplest change requires time to take hold and replace old ways of thinking and behaving. A concern I hear from mental health professionals is that too often parents come to them in crisis with their child, wanting a quick fix. The reality is that thought and behavior patterns that took years to develop do not yield to hours of intermittent therapy or coaching. Lasting changes require significant, long-term, commitment.

And now, it's confession time: I am the mom in the story that opened the book. That is an account written by my college-age daughter about the way she remembers many mornings during high school.

Yikes!

So even though I live and breathe this stuff, and know enough about it to write a book, I still struggle with the ups and downs of parenting, just like everyone. But I'm trying. I'm improving. I'm better today than I was yesterday, and I'll try to be even better tomorrow. This is all we can ask of ourselves, and it is all our children want from us.

Acknowledgments

THIS WILL OUT ME as the huge book nerd that I am, but I look forward to reading the acknowledgments at the end of books. It's true! I'm curious to know *how* someone came to construct a story or share their thoughts. Maybe I needed assurance, before I ventured to write my own book, that you don't just wake up one day and churn out the perfect manuscript.

I wrote *The Disintegrating Student* because I found myself repeating so much of the same information, over and over again, to interested parties who were intrigued and wanted to know more. It's not a stretch to say that the inspiration for this book came from decades of incubation. Years of indulging my interests in child development, education, and parenting. These passions inspired me to create The Balanced Student, which led me to write the book. Funny how life works.

I'm not sure I would ever have gotten into the rhythm of writing without advice from the writers in my life, Meredith Trotta and Kat Pattillo. Meredith advised me to write to my audience (parents) just as I would talk to them. And Kat told me to stop worrying about my words and write anything that came to mind without filtering. My husband and Kat also agreed to navigate school mornings without me so I could get some writing in before the start of the workday. Seven weeks later I had a 60,000+ word manuscript.

Roughly 20,000 of those words hit the road as my developmental editor Deborah Bancroft, "unspiraled" and shaped my convoluted draft into a cohesive, concise book. A talented high school student, Quinn McKeever, designed the original book cover. And I received helpful feedback and copyediting from my talented student intern, Katia Sergeeva.

A big thank-you to my first readers: Greg Becker, Marilee Hamilton, Susan Keenan, Carolyn Lambert, Ashley Loyd, Conner Martin, Beth O'Brien Burke, Kat Pattillo, Maddie Pattillo, Pat Pattillo, Ryan Pattillo, Tom Pattillo, Lisa Reid, Sarah Rhodes, Kelly Ryan, Krista Smith, Kellie Taylor, Ken Taylor, Riley Welch, Amy Whittall, and Colt Whittall.

Less than a year after I self-published, editor Denise Silvestro from Kensington Publishing Corp. reached out to me, believing that this book and its message needed to reach a wider audience. It has been an absolute dream to work with Denise, publicist Ann Pryor, and publisher Lynn Cully.

Thank you to all of my coworkers at Peachtree Psychology who support me in so many ways. And a special thank-you to Susan Keenan for having a vision for my work and asking me to be part of something great.

Beyond their support as first readers, my "Marble Jar" friendships with Susan Keenan, Kellie Taylor, Marilee Hamilton, and Beth O'Brien Burke have been as important to me as the air I breathe. I am beyond grateful for their support and inspiration, both personally and professionally.

I want to thank my parents, Ron and Connie Jannot, for showing me how to be a person in this world, and to live with integrity. Their love, support, and encouragement know no limit.

A huge thank-you to my husband, Tom Pattillo, for being a rock of support, tolerant as hell, and my best friend. He was an instrumental part of crafting the final manuscript, and always found a way to care on the days I found it hard to.

To my son, Jason Pattillo, who never took a breath outside my body, yet taught me more about myself than anyone—ever.

And finally, to my children, Ryan Pattillo, Maddie Pattillo, and Kat Pattillo—thank you for the privilege of being your mom. You've taught me how to be better. You've taught me what's important. You are my heart.

Helpful Resources and Recommended Reading

FOR READERS INTERESTED in learning more about the topics explored in this book, I've compiled this list of resources. This list is not comprehensive; these are the books I found to be most valuable in my work and research.

As of this writing, all of these books are available through most book retailers and public libraries. Websites may change over time; in case of a broken or missing link, try a quick internet search to be redirected.

Adolescent Brain Development

*Jensen, Frances E. *The Teenage Brain: A Neuroscientist's Survival Guide to Raising Adolescents and Young Adults.* HarperCollins Publishers, 2015.

---

* TED talk by author available. Search TED libraries: www.ted.com/talks and www.ted.com/watch/tedx-talks.

*Siegel, Daniel J. *Brainstorm: The Power and Purpose of the Teenage Brain.* Hachette India, 2014.

Walsh, David Allen, and Erin Walsh. *Why Do They Act That Way? A Survival Guide to the Adolescent Brain for You and Your Teen.* Atria Paperback, 2014.

Parenting

Abeles, Vicki. *Beyond Measure: How Our Obsession with Success, Homework, and Testing Threatens the Health and Happiness of Our Kids.* Simon & Schuster, 2015.

*Brown, Brené. *Daring Greatly: How the Courage to Be Vulnerable Transforms the Way We Live, Love, Parent, and Lead.* Penguin Life, 2015.

*Brown, Brené. *Dare to Lead: Brave Work, Tough Conversations, Whole Hearts.* Random House, 2018.

Chapman, Gary D. *The 5 Love Languages: The Secret to Love That Lasts.* Northfield Pub., 2015.

Levine, Madeline. *The Price of Privilege: How Parental Pressure and Material Advantage Are Creating a Generation of Disconnected and Unhappy Kids.* Harper, 2008.

Levine, Madeline. *Teach Your Children Well: Why Values and Coping Skills Matter More than Grades, Trophies, or "Fat Envelopes."* Harper Perennial, 2016.

*Lythcott-Haims, Julie. *How to Raise an Adult: Break Free of the Overparenting Trap and Prepare Your Kid for Success*. St. Martins Griffin, 2016.

Mogel, Wendy. *The Blessing of a B Minus: Using Jewish Teachings to Raise Resilient Teenagers*. Scribner, 2011.

Mogel, Wendy. *The Blessing of a Skinned Knee: Using Timeless Teachings to Raise Self-Reliant Children*. Scribner, 2016.

Skenazy, Lenore. *Free-Range Kids: How to Raise Safe, Self-Reliant Children (without Going Nuts with Worry)*. Jossey-Bass, 2010.

Stixrud, William R., and Ned Johnson. *The Self-Driven Child: The Science and Sense of Giving Your Kids More Control over Their Lives*. Viking, an imprint of Penguin Random House LLC, 2018.

Learning Strategies

Brown, Peter C. *Make It Stick: The Science of Successful Learning*. Belknap Harvard, 2018.

Carey, Benedict. *How We Learn: The Surprising Truth About When, Where, and Why It Happens*. Random House, 2015.

*Foer, Joshua. *Moonwalking with Einstein: A Journey Through Memory and the Mind*. Allen Lane, 2011.

Productivity and Achievement

*Bailey, Chris. *The Productivity Project: Accomplishing More by Managing Your Time, Attention, and Energy.* Crown Business, 2017.

*Duckworth, Angela. *Grit: Why Passion and Resilience Are the Secrets to Success.* Vermilion, 2017.

*Dweck, Carol S. *Mindset: The New Psychology of Success.* Robinson, 2012.

McKeown, Greg. *Essentialism: The Disciplined Pursuit of Less.* Virgin Books, 2014.

*Newport, Cal. *So Good They Can't Ignore You.* Piatkus Books, 2018.

*Newport, Cal. *How to Become a Straight-A Student: The Unconventional Strategies Real College Students Use to Score High While Studying Less.* Broadway Books, 2007.

*Newport, Cal. *How to Be a High School Superstar: A Revolutionary Plan to Get into College by Standing Out (Without Burning Out).* Broadway Books, 2010.

*Pink, Daniel H. *Drive: The Surprising Truth About What Motivates Us.* Canongate, 2011.

*Pink, Daniel H. *When: The Scientific Secrets of Perfect Timing.* Random House, 2018.

"Race to Nowhere: The Film, The Movement." *Race to Nowhere*, www.racetonowhere.com.

*Vanderkam, Laura. *168 Hours: You Have More Time Than You Think*. Penguin, 2011.

Sleep and Screens

*Randall, David K. *Dreamland: Adventures in the Strange Science of Sleep*. W.W. Norton & Company, 2013.

"Screenagers Movie: Growing up in the Digital Age." *Screenagers*, www.screenagersmovie.com.

"Sleep Research & Education." *National Sleep Foundation*, www.sleepfoundation.org.

*Twenge, Jean M. *IGen: Why Today's Super-Connected Kids Are Growing Up Less Rebellious, More Tolerant, Less Happy, and Completely Unprepared for Adulthood, and What That Means for the Rest of Us*. Atria Books, 2018.

Connect with U(s)

Visit us online at
KensingtonBooks.com
to read more from your favorite authors, see books
by series, view reading group guides, and more.

for sneak peeks, chances to win books and prize packs,
and to share your thoughts with other readers.

facebook.com/kensingtonpublishing
twitter.com/kensingtonbooks

Tell us what you think!

To share your thoughts, submit a review,
or sign up for our eNewsletters, please visit:
KensingtonBooks.com/TellUs.